email
for business
H A N D B O O K

Published by The TMTE Group, Sydney, Australia. Postal address: PO Box 1065 Darlinghurst NSW 1300. Street address: Level 1, 66 Oxford Street, Darlinghurst NSW 2010. Ph +61 2 9331 6611. Fax +61 2 9331 6149. http://www.tmte.com.au Email service@ecommercetoday.com.au

National Library of Australia Cataloguing-in-Publication reference:

1. Business - Computer network resources. 2. Electronic mail systems. 3. Electronic commerce. 4. Internet marketing. I. O'Shea, Peter. II. Title: Email For Business Handbook. 658.800285

ISBN: 0 646 38419 8

Printed in Australia

First published February 2000

CREDITS

Editor
Peter O'Shea

Assistant Editor
Daisy Hoffmann

Production Director
Jeremy Soh

Cover Design
Jenny Esdaile

Graphic Designers
Jenny Esdaile, Maxine Lloyd

Sales Director
Sue Mitchell

Publisher
Christopher Cormack

Contributing writers: Mark S. Ackerman, Richard Alston, Elizabeth Barnett, Rod Brooks, Lorrie Faith Cranor, Shelley Dempsey, Michael Dodge, Rob Edwards, Jim Fitzsimons, Andy Harris, Jim Heath, Simone Hewett, Matt Hockin, Paul Hoffman, David Jones, Peter Knight, Brian A. LaMacchia, Elaine Lawrence, Peter Leonard, Ben Macklin, Rob McMillan, Chris Morris, Tim O'Connor, Kevin O'Rourke, Tim Phillipps, Jeannie Rea, Joseph Reagle, Troy Rollo, Barry Saiff, Brendan Scott, Ann Slater, Jim Sterne, Lia Timson, Eric Ward.

Contributing organisations: AFP Technology, Arnold Bloch Leibler, AT&T, Australian Computer Emergency Response Team, Australian Direct Marketing Association, Australian Privacy Commissioner, Australian Bureau of Statistics, Australian Business Advisers, Australian Securities and Investments Commission, Baltimore Technologies, Brightmail, Coalition Against Unsolicited Bulk Email, Clayton Utz, Content Technologies, Corrs Chambers Westgarth, Dunhill Madden Butler, EmU Tcch, Epigraphx, ePrivacy, Forrester Research, GartnerGroup, Gilbert&Tobin, Information and Privacy Commissioner of Ontario Canada, InterBiz Solutions, Internet Mail Consortium, Manufacturing, Science and Finance Union UK, Massachusetts Institute of Technology, MessageMedia, Microsoft Corp., Multimedia Marketing Group, Morgan&Banks, National Archives of Australia, NetWizards, NSW Council for Civil Liberties, PricewaterhouseCoopers, Sterling Software, Target Marketing, Telstra Corp., Trend Micro, University of California, University of Technology, Sydney, URLwire, Viacorp, Victorian University of Technology, World Wide Web Consortium, Yahoo! Australia and NZ, Yellow Pages.

CONTENTS

CONTENTS

CONTENTS

Kana offers the most comprehensive suite of online customer communication products for managing the entire customer lifecycle, including inbound and outbound email, web-based customer self-service, web forms, real-time messaging and voice over the internet.

Kana's suite of online communication products includes solutions for e-business marketing, sales and service.

Kana Connect is the electronic direct marketing solution that enables e-businesses to pro-actively deliver individually targeted messages to increase the lifetime value of customers. The application enables marketers to profile, target and engage customers in one-to-one conversations through permission-based, email communication.

Kana Notify extends customer retail experience by automating, customising and managing transaction-related communications such as order status and receipts, and helps to reduce customer service inquiries by sending pro-active messages.

Kana Realtime is an e-commerce solution that enables companies to engage in one-to-one realtime communications with customers to generate higher sales conversions. The solution's live two-way web-based dialogue between the company and customer provides immediate online sales assistance to help companies turn browsers into buyers, reduce shopping cart abandonment, cross-sell and up-sell during the sales cycle, and reduce sales service costs.

Kana Response is a high performance email customer service solution that enables e-businesses to respond to, monitor, and manage high volumes of customer service inquiries. The main components of the system include workflow automation tools, a knowledge base, and a database to track all activity.

Kana Classify is a powerful, advanced and highly scalable artificial intelligence technology that enables automatic responses to customer e-mail. The system's dynamic customer database provides an efficient system to store customer information, identify needs and pro-actively target individuals with personalised messages.

Kana Assist is an online self-service solution that improves the customer experience by delivering context-sensitive answers to customer questions directly on the website — allowing customers to quickly and conveniently obtain answers to their questions without the intervention of a customer service representative.

Kana's solutions are proven, with more than 250 customers, ranging from Global 2000 enterprises to newly established internet-based businesses. Kana customers include: eBay, eToys, priceline.com, Lycos, Chase Manhattan Bank, Ford Motor Company and Northwest Airlines.

Kana Communications can be found at http://www.kana.com/home.html

EmU Tech

EmU Tech Pty Ltd is an Australian based company established in 1998 to address the issues of email abuse facing Australian and international government and corporate entities. EmU Tech have developed email traffic management and policy enforcement software to protect organisations from internal and external email risks. Emu Tech and its resellers also provide specialised consulting services on email policy. http://www.emutech.com.au

eGain

eGain Communications is a leading solution provider for e-commerce customer communication. eGain develops, markets and supports a comprehensive suite of integrated customer communications solutions including email, real-time, campaigns, self-service and voice that help eCommerce companies establish profitable, long-term relationships with their customers. eGain's solutions are available through onsite deployments or through the eGain Hosted Network, the world's largest network for eCommerce customer service. Companies use eGain solutions to build customer loyalty, to convert online visitors to online buyers and to leverage customer information. For more information about eGain, please visit http://www.egain.com

ABOUT THE PUBLISHER

The Email for Business Handbook is an initiative of The TMTE Group, a 100% Australian owned advertising, design and publishing company, based in Sydney, Australia. Its premier e-commerce publication E-Commerce Today, provides a weekly news service published in hardcopy and on the web, and a monthly magazine published in hardcopy and, as of early this year, also online.

Launched in July 1998, E-Commerce Today is still Australia's only independent news service and magazine specifically reporting on trends in e-commerce business issues in the Australian marketplace. In the past 12 months, readership of both the news service and the magazine has grown dramatically, its success primarily due to the Australian editorial focus, quality content, a fully searchable archive database on the website, and independent reporting.

The collective industry intelligence gathered led The TMTE Group to conclude that the Australian market is demanding more information about email, its applications and how to incorporate it strategically into marketing, customer relationship management and internal use.

As this handbook reveals, email is the greatest use of the internet, yet there is very little in the marketplace specifically about this dynamic and revolutionary tool.

The principle purpose of the Email for Business Handbook is to raise the awareness of the marketing, ethical, consumer, privacy, legal and security issues involved with email use, of which there are many, and to arm business readers with information to take their business forward into the challenging information age.

We hope you find it as useful and illuminating as we did when compiling it.

Please provide feedback and see our website –
http://www.ecommercetoday.com.au/emailhandbook/

FOREWORD

Electronic commerce offers considerable new business opportunities and benefits in terms of cost savings for business. It empowers consumers, giving them more information on which to base their decisions, more choice in their source of supply and a greater ability to demand customised goods and services.

It enables governments to improve the quality and effectiveness of services to the community and to be more responsive to community needs.

Email is a major tool in the use of e-commerce and, used properly and ethically, it can improve communication and build closer relationships with existing and new customers.

To be able to take advantage of these opportunities, business and government need to be informed about the trading environment in the online world and the use of email, as well as the challenges and changes that business and government need to address to make the most of them.

The Commonwealth Government is actively engaged with industry in supporting projects in areas as diverse as the wool, pharmaceutical and automotive industries to ensure the benefits of e-commerce are spread throughout the economy.

There is a clear priority to support an environment conducive to the widespread use of e-commerce in Australia that demonstrates the business case, targets barriers and maximises the efficiency dividend for the economy.

Richard Alston, Minister for Communications, Information Technology and the Arts.

Internet Growth and Email Use: In Short, It's Exploding

Introduction

E stimating how many internet users exist worldwide is obviously like trying to estimate the number of people on the planet. The number is just too big and changing too quickly for an accurate answer. But some have tried to make a close guess.

US-based Nua Surveys, which publishes research from myriad sources relating to internet use, says an "educated guess" is that, as of September 1999, from observing many of the published surveys over the previous two years, the number of online users was 201 million.

Between 1993 and 1997, the number of computers connected to the internet grew from one million to 20 million and, by 2001, that figure is expected to rise to 120 million, according to the Department of Foreign Affairs and Trade.

Some have estimated that the value of global internet commerce ranges from 1.3 to 3.3% of global gross domestic product by 2001. A report commissioned by Australia's National Office for the Information Economy estimated that Australia's gross domestic product could be boosted by an extra 2.7% by 2007 – roughly the equivalent to one year's economic growth – if Australian businesses adopt the use of e-commerce.

That study, E-Commerce: Beyond 2000, projected that e-commerce would also raise consumption by 3.2% by 2007 and increase real wages by around 3.5%, due to improved labour productivity.

Email use has been found by myriad researchers – and businesses – to be the top reason people go online. The 1999 PricewaterhouseCoopers Consumer Technology Survey released last September found that the preferred online activity of those who access the internet from home in the US wasn't doing research or shopping, but sending and receiving email.

That survey found that email had surpassed research as the major reason for US consumers to go online (48% compared to 28%). In the UK, however, consumers equally used the internet for email (39%) and research (39%). Both the Germans and French primarily go online for research purposes (at 14%).

In Australia, the Australian Bureau of Statistics has found that email was found to be the main reason people logged on – along with research. A survey in May 1999 found email was used by 92% of businesses with access to the internet. The proportion of businesses using email closely matched the proportion of businesses with web browser capabilities (29% and 26% of all businesses respectively).

Other researchers in the UK have found that email is now the dominant form of communication between companies. They also found, as an article in this chapter reveals, it can cut costs – by as much as 30%. When taken into consideration with the dramatic rise in internet use, email is moving in rapidly where paper (and even faxes) once were.

The boom in the use of this new tool is inspiring a whole new range of services, ranging from Internet Service Providers to email directories. In Australia these include email-it.net.au and worldemail.com (a global company), which allow individuals or businesses to enter their email address and search for others who have entered their address in the directory.

Searches and entries are typically free as service providers make their revenue by advertising on their website. However, there are ethical considerations relating to unsolicited email (as an entire chapter later in this handbook outlines). Many email directories are aware of this and usually require users to promise not to send unsolicited email marketing material. Telstra's White Pages claims to have 26,000 email and internet addresses in its directory.

While this chapter discusses the key facts and figures on internet users and email users in Australia, its key trading partners and around the world, others chapters in this handbook discuss the legal issues, privacy concerns, and ethical issues, aiming to illuminate your business' path through this new boom.

Online Users – World by Region

Canada & USA	112.4 million
Europe	47.15 million
Asia/Pacific	33.61 million
Latin America	5.29 million
Africa	1.72 million
Middle East	0.88 million

SOURCE: Nua Surveys, Sept 1999. Online figures were adults and children who accessed the internet at least once during the three months prior to being surveyed. http://www.nua.ie/surveys/

REFERENCE: Nua Internet Surveys World Total "educated guess"

http://www.nua.ie/surveys/how_many_online/index.html

DID YOU KNOW?

Among all small businesses in Australia, just under half (43%) used email to communicate with clients, customers and other business contacts, according to the annual Yellow Pages Small Business Index survey of computer technology and e-commerce, released in May 1999. For medium-sized businesses, according to the survey, the figure was 84%.

The Use of Email by Business in Australia

Email is the leading business use of the internet in Australia. As Australian businesses embrace the information age they are doing so utilising the digital era's fastest and most popular communications power tool. Email is cheap, secure, virtually instantaneous and quickly overtaking the fax as choice for business correspondence.

For businesses that have already implemented technology and have their computers online, email is by far the main use of the web. In a study of business use of information technology, 1997-1998, the Australian Bureau of Statistics (ABS) found that email was used by 92% of the 29% of all Australian businesses with internet access — more than a quarter of all businesses.

This was up from findings in a 1998 report released by the Federal Government, Stats.Electronic Commerce, which reported that more than 80% of firms predominantly used the internet for email and research purposes.

The use of email and the internet grows with the size of the business. The annual Yellow Pages Small Business Index survey of computer technology and e-commerce, released in May 1999, found that among all small businesses in Australia, just under half (43%) use email to communicate with clients, customers and other business contacts, according. For medium-sized businesses, according to the survey, the figure is 84% (See table).

This report also noted that the usage of both email and the internet is highest in the mining industry (46%), the business services sector and the communication services industry (both 45%). The building and construction industry has the lowest proportion of email access. The Yellow Pages report also found that more than half of small and medium-sized business proprietors have internet access in their home as well as at work.

The most common locations for people to access the internet is in their home, followed closely by their workplace. According to the ABS, around 84% of adults who accessed the internet at home in 1997-98 did so at least once a week, compared with 76% of adults accessing the internet at work and 24% of adults accessed the internet from sites other than home or work.

Email (along with research) is also the most common use of the internet at home. The ABS found that, in May 1999, almost half (47%) of all Australian households (just over 3.2 million households) had a home computer and just over 22% of all households (or 1.5 million households) had home internet access. This figure had risen 14% compared to May 1998.

For some industries business and personal email address have become mandatory, as much of a necessity as a phone number, and according to Telstra there were around 26,000 email and internet addresses listed in the White Pages in 1999. Telstra believes that 90-95% of those addresses are business or government related. Email and web addresses are now routinely added to the White Pages' CD-Rom and the internet site. Telstra says while the most popular information required is phone numbers and addresses, requests for email addresses are now not too far behind.

Email use by business size

Business Size	Using Email (%)
1-2 Employees	38%
3-4 Employees	50%
5-9 Employees	46%
10-19 Employees	65%
20-100 Employees	82%
101-200 Employees	94%
Small Businesses Total	43%
Medium Businesses Total	84%
All Businesses	46%

SOURCE: Yellow Pages® Small Business Index 1999.

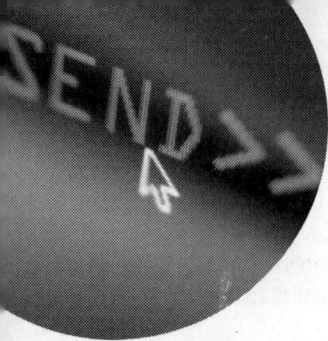

How Australia Compares to the Rest of the World

Country	Date of Statistic Collected	Percentage of the Population Online
Australia	1/99	24%
Sweden	5/99	41%
USA	5/99	37%
Norway	5/99	37%
Netherlands	3/99	14%
Germany	3/99	10%
France	6/98	7%

SOURCE: NUA Surveys, drawing on multiple studies. http://www.nua.ie

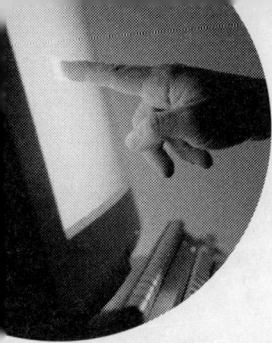

Regional Email Use Among Australia's Key Trading Partners

Australia's top trading partners, according to Austrade, are Japan, the United States, the Republic of Korea, New Zealand and China, all of which are, like Australia, in the midst of an email explosion.

The use of email has soared in recent years and, globally, web use is expected to keep on growing at an exponential rate. For example, according to Internet Asia, Hanmail Net Online, a South Korean portal site offering free email services, had to wait a year and a half to get one million registered users but by June 1999 it was getting one million new users every five months.

The Asia Pacific Economic Cooperation (APEC) Telecommunications Working Group (TEL) released results in October 1999 of a global survey conducted by PricewaterhouseCoopers. Conducted in all 21 APEC countries over four months, the survey was completed by more than 1,300 SMEs (defined as having fewer than 500 employees).

It found expanding customers and markets was seen as the driving force in e-commerce adoption by responding SMEs. Over 90% of these companies saw building customer relationships through improved customer service and information exchange as an important benefit of their e-commerce initiatives.

Japan

- There are over 18 million internet users in Japan. – Nikkei NetBusiness Survey, September 1999.

US

- Email is the primary activity for those in the US using the internet, used by nearly 80% of those with home internet access. – US Government.

- The typical US worker receives over 200 emails per day, compared to the typical UK worker, who receives 171 emails per day. – Survey reported by US-based e-commerce and internet-based research firm NUA.

Sending email had surpassed researching information as the primary reason for accessing the internet, according to a technology study by PricewaterhouseCoopers in September 1999. A similar report in 1998 found that researching information was the primary reason.

The report also found that the number of people spending most of their time sending or receiving email jumped from 27% in 1998 to 48% in 1999. Of those accessing the internet at home, 77.9% used it to email and, of that group, 93.6% used email to communicate with family and friends.

South Korea

- In South Korea, at the end of April 1999, four million people were online and five million were expected to be online by the end of 1999. – Samsung Economic Research Institute.

According to the Samsung Economic Research Institute (SERI), there has been a tenfold increase in the amount of Koreans using the internet in the last three years. A survey by the Korea Information Culture Center found around 87% of Koreans have visited an online shopping mall at least once and of those, 51.2% have bought something online.

New Zealand

- There were more than 561,000 internet users in New Zealand at the end of 1998. This represents about 16% of the total population. – Survey reported by US-based e-commerce and internet-based research firm NUA.

China

- Four million people had internet access in China in 1999 and 20 million are expected to have internet access by 2003. – Chinese Ministry of the Information Industry.

Taiwan

- The number of internet users has grown by 50% every six months in the last three years and now numbers 4.2 million, according to a study conducted by the FIND Institute for Information Industries and commissioned by the Department of Industrial Technology. In 1999, Taiwan's online population grew from 3 million in January to more than 4 million in early September.

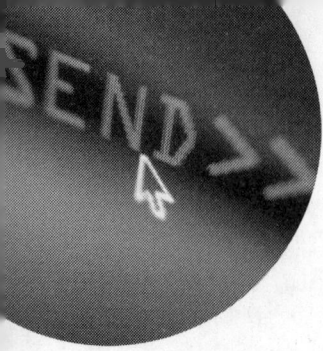

European Email Use Catching Up on the US

The UK is behind the USA, Canada and Australia in respect to the percentage of population with regular internet access – but the UK Government wants this to change.

Its Competitiveness White Paper, released last year, set the target of increasing the number of micro-companies and SMEs wired up to the digital marketplace by making use of external networking technologies such as external email, websites and Electronic Data Interchange (EDI) from 350,000 at the beginning of 1998 to one million by 2002.

This target was prompted, in part, by findings of a 1999 study which aimed to benchmark the levels of ownership, usage and understanding of information and communication technologies by companies in G7 nations (France, Germany, Japan, UK, USA, Italy and Canada) found that the UK is also behind the Scandinavian economies of Sweden, Norway and Finland.

Commissioned by the UK Department of Trade and Industry, the 1999 International Benchmarking Study, undertaken by UK-based Spectrum Strategy Consultants, found the overall proportion of companies using email has grown in all countries.

In most countries more than 70% of companies used email, with the exception of France and Italy, where business use of email was 51% and 48% respectively. Germany experienced the greatest jump in the use of email, with the percentage of German companies using it up by 25% in 1999 from 1998.

In all countries the overall proportion of companies using external email was greater than those using it internally. Companies in Canada, the UK, the US and Japan had similar levels of uptake of email. Despite the greater use of external email, internal email was used more often, the study found.

The most frequent users of internal and external email were Canada, the UK and the US. Italian businesses use email least frequently of the G7 nations.

Companies Using Email External and Internal (large, SMEs and "micro" companies).

Country	1999	1998	1997
Canada	83%	N/A	N/A
Japan	79%	72%	51%
UK	75%	63%	52%
Germany	73%	48%	43%
US	72%	65%	56%
France	51%	41%	32%
Italy	48%	N/A	N/A

SOURCE: Spectrum ICT Survey of Businesses by NOP Research Group. http://www.nop.co.uk

Spectrum found that, of the companies it interviewed, most considered the introduction of email as having a positive impact on their business relationships. The ease and speed of communications was the biggest reason cited.

One company, ASLA Ltd, a provider to the wholesale travel trade, said it had cut communication costs by 30%. Some companies, however, said that excessive use of internal email particularly by employees was having a negative impact on business productivity.

Email - The Most Popular Use of the Internet in the US

In the United States, where much of e-commerce originates, around one third of small businesses — often regarded as the driving force of an economy — are online. According to a recent study commissioned by Prodigy Biz Corp., a subsidiary of Prodigy Communications Corp, an additional 40% of small businesses without websites (around 2.1 million) expect to be on the internet by about July this year.

Primary uses of the internet cited were: promoting to prospects (69%), e-commerce (57%), providing better customer service (48%), competing with other businesses (46%) and communicating with employees (11%). Much of this was done using email.

According to research firm IDC, nearly two-thirds of all US businesses with a computer have email. Further, about 15% of the US population has access to email and, as users become more accustomed to the internet, the use of email increases on average to about 25 messages a day, according to US online media and advertising company ActivMedia.

In the US, like Australia, email is the most popular use of the net. The PricewaterhouseCoopers' 1999 Consumer Technology survey found that email had replaced research as the primary reason why people in the US go online. Forty-eight percent of US users surveyed mid last year said they went online for email while 28% said they went online to research. Last year those figures were exactly in reverse.

Internet and Email Use Patterns in the US

- Internet access in US homes increased sharply, up by nearly 60% to 43%.

- Consumers in the US also spend almost twice as much time on the internet: 5.3 hours in a typical week.

- Asked what they do when online 48% of American consumers with home access said communicating.

- Email has surpassed research (28%) as the primary reason to go online.

- Asked what they would do if the internet did not exist, the majority of the Americans (70%) said they would watch television or read.

- Americans (32%) are most concerned with the speed with which they can operate on the internet.

- The number of Americans unwilling to shop online was 19%, down from 30% last year.

SOURCE: The PricewaterhouseCoopers Consumer Technology Survey, October 1999.

How Email Use in Europe Compares to the US

Email is now the primary means of delivery for many kinds of business document, displacing post and facsimile as the primary means of business document distribution.

In March 1999 UK-based AFP Technologies surveyed 139 European and US firms — mainly multinationals with an average of 50,000 employees. The survey looked at overall trends in email use, differences between the US and European companies' use of email and the future use of email.

"Already email accounts for 38% of all document traffic (internal and external)," the company concluded. "US companies are both more cost conscious than their European counterparts and more aware of the benefits email can bring to bear on customer service. Shortened lead times for customer communications was mentioned by 95% of US respondents as a motivating factor in email deployment, but by 63% of the European companies that took part in the survey."

Key Findings:

• 38% of all documents now go by email

Thirty-eight percent of all documents and 54% of internal documents are sent by email. In a significant minority of cases (27%), more than half of all document traffic and as much as three-quarters of internal traffic uses the email network.

• 17.5% of messages have attachments

As many as one in six of email messages are sent with file attachments. The figure is remarkably high – twice that recorded in some other surveys – but still points to enormous growth in the use of email as a postal service for information of all kinds.

Europe Closing the Gap on the US

The gap between US companies with their ready acceptance of new technologies and their more conservative European counterparts is closing fast. US companies remain more sophisticated in their use of the technology and, perhaps as a consequence, have higher expectations of what it can deliver.

Now is Now the Primary Medium for Written Communications Within Companies

There is unsurprisingly a marked difference in the pattern of email use for internal versus external document distribution. Email messages have almost entirely replaced the written or typed memo and significant volumes of other internal documents, including financial instruments and administrative forms are exchanged electronically and no longer on paper.

A Growing Medium for Communications Between Companies

The proportion of outward-bound documents carried by email is lower, but a still substantial 24% of all external correspondence is now conducted this way. Where paper continues to change hands it is for cultural reasons (because customers or suppliers request it), for legal reasons, or because of insufficient penetration of technology.

Customer Service the Primary Driver

The driving force behind the increased reliance on email is the belief that it shortens lead times for customer communications, according to 63% of the European and 95% of the US companies in the survey. Many respondents also saw email as the key to streamlining business processes. Cost effectiveness is a welcome by-product of email adoption, but not the main motivating factor.

Conclusions

- Attachments seen as the key to document delivery. Attachments are a vitally important part of the picture. Attachments enable many traditional objections to email to be overcome.

- Documents can be to word-processor or pre-press standards and printed out without loss of quality. Virtually anything that can be created on a computer can be sent as an attachment.

- Email, with its limited character set and virtually non-existent formatting capabilities, is ill-suited as a medium for documents that will later be edited or otherwise re-used. Attached files can usually be edited using a local copy of the program used to create them.

- Email can be an equally bad choice where the requirement is for documents that the recipient cannot change – such as invoices. Attachments can include files as PDFs, which can be viewed and printed but not edited.

- Only the most rudimentary forms can be sent as basic email messages. Attachments make it viable for using email for complex forms.

- Email is a poor medium for delivering data. Attachments allow data to be sent in a variety of rich formats including spreadsheets and database files.

The Problem With Attachments

While few companies question the value of attachments, they come at a price. Among the main concerns are security and confidentiality, the threat of network overload from vastly increased file traffic (an attachment can be thousands of times the size of a typical email message), and cost of providing extra storage.

Enabling Service for Other Applications

Rather than being regarded as an application in its own right, email is increasingly seen as an enabling service for the automation of business processes, for document management and for workflow applications.

Moves to Better Internal Systems Create Pressure for Better External Ones

Moves by companies to put their own houses in order, and reduce paper in favour of more efficient electronic media, are providing a further boost to email. Just as they no longer wish to move tons of paper around their organisations, they no longer wish to have tons more delivered by customers and suppliers. Where once it was for paper, the de facto requirement will shortly be for electronic copies of documentation. Rationalisation of internal systems and processes by trading partners creates a pull effect which forces the companies they do business with to follow suit.

Low Penetration of Email Among Consumers Restraining Growth

The use of email for marketing literature and customer correspondence is growing rapidly but mainly in the business-to-business sphere. Written communications between businesses and consumers are still largely conducted on paper. The main reasons are relatively low penetration of email among consumers and a lack of email directory information in consumer databases. This will change with the spread of the internet and the proliferation of affordable devices that can access it. But consumer resistance to technology and the threat of a flood-tide of junk messages could both severely limit the speed of acceptance of email.

Constraints

Penetration of email inside and outside the company is the most important factor constraining the development of email cultures. Customer resistance to electronic documents is another factor. Concerns about increased network traffic and consequent extra costs tend to be offset by the perception of cost-benefits elsewhere.

Growth of Email Threatens Post and Fax

The growth of email is at the expense of other document distribution media. Both post and fax are expected to experience dramatic declines over the next five years. In the case of fax, the decline could be fatal.

This article was reprinted with permission by AFP Technology. Based in the UK, it specialises in the development of electronic document design, management and output systems. The full report of "Email Culture: Europe and the US" is available at their website http://www.afptech.com

Summary of Key Findings

- 38% of all documents now go by email
- 17.5% of messages have attachments
- Europe closing the gap on the US
- Now the primary medium for written communications within companies
- A growing medium for communications between companies
- Moves to better internal systems create pressure for better external ones
- Low penetration of email among consumers restraining growth

References

Australian Bureau of Statistics: http://www.abs.gov.au

APEC's E-Commerce Task Force: http://www.dfat.gov.au/apec/ecom/

Final survey results of the APEC survey **Electronic Commerce Study on E-Commerce** in APEC's 21 member countries: http://www.apecsec.org.sg

Department of Foreign Affairs and Trade's reports released in February 1999 outlining the growth and use of e-commerce generally in Australia and internationally: Clearway on the New Silk Road: The Use of Electronic Commerce by Australia Business; and Driving Forces on the New Silk Road: International Business and Policy Trends: http://www.dfat.gov.au/nsr

Nua Surveys, reporting its own and other organisations' internet-related survey and research results: http://www.nua.ie/surveys/

Statistics.com, an online database and information hub for a range of world statistics relating to a wide range of topics. Also has information on statistics software, as well as about statistics analysis, data analysis and short courses in statistics: http://www.statistics.com/

National Office for the Information Economy's **study on the economic impact of E-Commerce: Beyond 2000**. An executive summary can be downloaded from http://www.noie.gov.au/ecom/HOME/Policy/Economic_Impacts_Study/economic_imp acts_study.html

Stats.Electronic Commerce, a Federal Government report released in April 1998 on the use of e-commerce in Australia (also discusses email use): http://www.noie.gov.au/ecom/HOME/Publications/publications.html

Taking The Plunge: Business Attitudes to E-Commerce, a report by the National Office for the Information Economy and the Federal Government-funded AeBN (now Ausenet) on small and medium-sized businesses' attitudes to e-commerce: http://www.dcita.gov.au/infoind/index.html

Internet research firm IDC: http://www.idc.com

Links to **OECD reports on SME use and e-commerce,** The Economic and Social Impact of Electronic Commerce: http://www.ottawaoecdconference.org/english/homepage.html

AFP Technologies: http://www.afptech.co.uk/afptech/htmlsite/intro_e.htm

Robert H'obbes' Zakon's Timeline: a history of ARPAnet (Internet's predecessor) including email. Includes references to recent internet history books with background on email's history: http://www.isoc.org/zakon/

History of the internet in Australia on Roger Clarke's home page: http://www.anu.edu.au/people/Roger.Clarke/II/OzIHist.html

Opt-In Permission Marketing: Ask Nicely and You Shall Receive

Introduction
Direct Email – The New Way to Target Market

By Lia Timson

A s anyone will tell you, the most important element of marketing is the consumer. And knowing them well, is the secret to communicating with them in a relevant matter.

Mass advertisers have spent billions of dollars over the years trying to get to know their target market better through quantitative and qualitative research. Even today, for every commercial that goes to air, there's an advertiser somewhere praying that it will hit the mark with at least some of its passive target.

Direct email does away with all that. For, the very nature of emailing implies an active involvement by the recipient, be it in supplying his or her email address – as in permission marketing – or in simply opening the message to read its contents.

It's active marketing and, because of that, the responsibility born by the marketer is perhaps much greater than that of the advertiser who simply shouts to the wind and hopes somebody will hear it.

In email marketing, you are communicating directly with a potential customer. In their house, their work, their private "for your eyes only" space. It is a conversation between two people via the computer screen. Your behaviour here should be no different than if you were talking to a client in person. You're representing a firm, a brand. Your reputation lies in your approach and presentation.

Direct emailing without recipient consent is considered spamming, a subject much debated in more advanced internet circles such as the United States and European Union, where legislation is in place to attempt to stop it and marketers can be sued over breaches of privacy and fraud.

However, in Australia, direct emailing is still in its infancy. Scott McClellan, communications director of the Australian Direct Marketing Association (ADMA), says marketers are only just beginning to explore the internet as a marketing medium.

"Not many of the established direct marketing community are using email extensively as a direct marketing tool yet. The ones that are, use it more for customer service," he says.

By established community, McClellan means those marketers that value their hard-earned customer relationship. For them, threading carefully onto the email world is a matter of brand reputation survival.

According to www.consult there are approximately 4.5 million email accounts in Australia, of which one million is free of charge from services such as Hotmail and Yahoo!Mail. About 50% of the total is a second email address at the work or home of a recipient.

This has implications for the marketer who wants to ensure its communication is both well received and not doubled-up. The process by which an email address can be acquired includes voluntary disclosure of the details by the consumer (they ask to be mailed specific information); gathering of addresses contained in webpages and gathering of addresses posted in newsgroups. The last two are usually compiled by intermediaries and sold to marketers without the recipient's knowledge or consent. Such lists can be widely obtained on CD-Rom for as little as $99.

More serious internet businesses are beginning to ask customers and email account holders whether they would like to receive further relevant information. This system is known as opt-in/opt-out.

Craig Lambert, Yahoo!'s advertising sales director, says the company follows the opt-in system exclusively. This means the answer to the question "do you want to receive further offers from Yahoo!?" is defaulted to a "no" tick. Consumers must actively select "yes" if they so wish.

"Permission is important because we don't want to abuse the user relationship. People get really annoyed with unsolicited offers and don't act on them," Lambert says.

Malcolm Auld, direct marketing guru and author of Direct Marketing Made Easy, says email marketing is an outstanding way of targeting. "Only as long as people have identified themselves willingly."

He says solicited communication works wonders for brand perception because the recipient enjoys the personal contact and respect shown in the relevant information. "But if you get it wrong it is more damaging [than other forms of marketing]," he adds.

Spamming is considered abominable in serious direct marketing circles. In the United States, there are a number of anti-spamming lobby groups, concerned not only with the invasion of privacy derived from being contacted by someone unwelcome, to sheer money-grabbing scams and fraud. The US Federal Trade Commission is also stepping up its enforcement activities and many anti-spamming organisations provide a forum through which complaints can be forwarded for investigation.

Similar legislation is not yet in place or underway in Australia. But, according to Peter Knight, partner at law firm Clayton Utz, voluntary codes of practice which include provisions for privacy and disclosure, such as that adopted by the ADMA and the ones proposed by the Internet Industry Association and the Australian Consumer Competition Commission (ACCC), will prove more useful than government regulation.

"When you look at spamming it is a question of degree. Some of it is offensive, but most of it is unsolicited junk mail. Interestingly enough, voluntary codes can be taken into account in the (Trade Practices Act) 4a paragraph in determination of whether there has been unconscionable conduct," Knight says.

Avoiding the annoyance factor is then, the secret to effective email marketing. "Think about what is appropriate and acceptable for these activities," says ADMA's McClellan. And you should be on your way to a fulfiling two-way communication with your customer.

Lia Timson is a Sydney-based freelance journalist and regular contributor to E-Commerce Today. http://www.ecommercetoday.com.au

---

DID YOU KNOW?

There are approximately 4.5 million email accounts in Australia, of which one million are free accounts. About 50% of the total was a second email address at the work or home of a recipient

Avoiding the Pitfalls in Email Marketing

By Chris Morris

mail is evolving into a ubiquitous, inexpensive channel for distributing information to customers. Indeed, GartnerGroup projects that more than 80% of enterprises that do direct marketing today will conduct at least one email marketing campaign by year-end 2001. However, there is likely to be significant consumer backlash: consumers accept junk mail as a fact of life. But they are far less tolerant about unsolicited email.

Email marketing is the practice of using outbound email to make customers (either businesses or consumers) aware of a company and its special promotions. It can be both cheaper and easier to track than direct mail or telemarketing, and for that reason more companies are trying it.

The cost of a piece of direct mail and an outbound telemarketing call can be significantly higher than the cost of an outbound email. In addition, there are a number of software products and services that can track email response rates to calculate Return on Investment (ROI).

Five Email Pitfalls

When used correctly, email is a valuable addition to the marketing mix. But enterprises considering email marketing should remember that it's better suited to customer retention and extension than customer acquisition. Five of the most common pitfalls companies encounter are:

Pitfall No. 1: Using email as if it were direct mail. For years marketers have been sending unsolicited direct mail to attract new customers. Many falsely assume email can be used to the same effect. However, the same prospects that consider junk mail a fact of life may protest bitterly when sent an unsolicited email, or "spam".

Tip: Enterprises should send email marketing messages only to current customers or to members of reputable lists who have stated they are willing to receive such messages. This may reduce the potential benefit of the mailing, but it also mitigates the risk.

Pitfall No. 2: Using email to bombard customers. The internet enables annoyed customers to identify a company's competitors (through search engines), compare a company with its competitors (through chat rooms), and, if necessary, begin doing business with a rival. Hence, enterprises must be careful not to irritate customers and avoid trying to increase mind share by overwhelming customers with email marketing.

Tip: Make customers feel they control the flow of information. If a customer decides they do not want to receive more marketing emails, consider more subtle methods (e.g., marketing messages in online billing statements and customer service updates).

Pitfall No. 3: Failing to prepare for customer response. It seems intuitive that increased promotional activity will increase response rates; however, many companies do not consider the effect of promotions on inbound email volume and Web activity. Organisations should look at typical direct mail response rates of one to 2% and assume that email response rates will be slightly higher, as customers only need to click on a link or hit "reply" to respond.

Tip: Enterprises must plan to manage the full life cycle of an outbound email marketing campaign. Email marketing will increase inbound activity, so marketers should consult customer service, sales, interactive, and information services departments before executing campaigns.

Pitfall No. 4: Failing to personalise the email. Several companies, notably Amazon.com, are incorporating sophisticated personalisation in email marketing messages. Amazon records a customer's past purchases and targets email marketing messages based on those purchases. This type of personalisation is a radical improvement over more common, superficial efforts to personalise email by simply including the customer's name in the message.

Customers are starting to expect companies to remember past interactions to improve future interactions. The difficulty of this task increases with the number of customers, the number of channels used, and the frequency of customer interaction. So smaller companies and pure-play internet companies will have an advantage over larger enterprises.

Tip: Leading enterprises should incorporate email marketing into a broader customer-relationship management strategy. While this presents additional challenges, it also increases the potential business benefits.

Pitfall No. 5: Neglecting to test campaigns. Several enterprises have suffered major embarrassment and customer dissatisfaction by failing to provide the resources needed to manage and operate an email campaign, or by failing to test their campaigns. For example, one inadvertently exposed the email addresses of all recipients on its distribution list, while another repeatedly sent the same message.

Tip: Enterprises must have the skills and resources to manage an email marketing campaign, and should test each campaign on a focus group prior to sending the entire campaign.

Chris Morris is a Vice President and Research Director based in GartnerGroup's Sydney office. For more information, email:
information.asiapacific@gartner.com

Building Community With Email Discussion Lists

By Matt Hockin

There is a lot of talk on the internet these days about big corporations constructing portal sites that "build community" and offer internet users a gateway or starting point to the net. This may have you wondering how you can compete with such well established companies and their highly visited sites for your very own piece of virtual real estate.

How does a smaller company, organisation, or even a home-based business, compete? How can you build your own community around your company to increase profits and build your business?

But smaller, savvy internet marketers are succeeding on internet. Small business, organisations, and even home-based businesses have an advantage and are well positioned to profit in this new internet medium. Larger companies are slow to adapt, while smaller marketers have adapted to this new frontier with ease and will grow as a result of their high level of awareness, hard work and marketing skill.

They become successful by providing valuable information. Information is irresistible. Information is what web surfers are looking for when they stumble on to commercial web sites. If you position yourself and your company as one of the internet's premiere information providers for your industry and niche, you will attract people who want to buy from your business.

One of the most effective tools for providing the information people are hungry for – and at the same time building community around your business – is with internet's most effective form of "push technology", that is, email.

What's even more powerful than email alone, is a moderated email discussion list of individuals all linked together with a common interest who share their experiences, information and opinions.

Equipped with a discussion list, your company can become "the source" of information that people are looking for in your particular industry. A discussion list will also serve as a support community of like-minded colleagues. This is especially good for you since people who are interested in your product or service will naturally gravitate to your site and/or list from links on the internet.

An example of how a moderated discussion list can help your business or organisation is Ray Gabriel's Association for International Business list http://www.earthone.com/

It gave his company credibility and a tremendous amount of word of mouth advertising. The list enabled him to reach many contacts for funding his non-profit organisation's goals. It was also a very satisfying way to meet people and help them find the information they needed for their businesses.

Nancy Roebke is another example of someone who moderates an email discussion list successfully. Nancy, a leading expert of how to use networking and relationship building as a way to market and grow your business, says her list is an excellent networking and marketing tool. The list is a place for women and men to discuss and exchange information about business issues.

She says the list (http://www.profnet.org/) takes a little time (about 1-2 hours a day) but generates a substantial amount of business and is well worth the effort. "Being a moderator of a discussion list is like being a leader of a community of people," she says.

Our own company, Multimedia Marketing Group (MMG) also started an email discussion list in 1995 called the "I-Sales Discussion List" to support people interested in learning how to market their products or services on the internet.

The email discussion list, accompanied by free information made available on the MMG's website, drew large amounts of targeted traffic and generated an impressive amount of word-of-mouth advertising and resulted in free publicity and a wealth of links for MMG.

To summarise the above points, you can build your business and beat the big corporations at the internet game by providing your market with the information they seek. A moderated email discussion list can be an internet marketer's most powerful tool for building community and profits.

Matt Hockin is with the US-based Multimedia Marketing Group, an online marketing agency with offices in London, Oregon and New York. The company can be found at http://www.mmgco.com

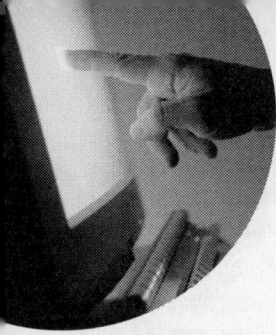

How to Maintain Human Relationships in the Digital World

By Rod Brooks

Business today relies on customer relationships. Products or services can often be rapidly copied or superseded, and there very often is a competitor somewhere prepared to offer a similar product for a lower price.

Don Peppers and Martha Rogers, US-based marketing gurus and authors of the book "The One-to-One Future", conclude: "No matter how creative and innovative your firm is the only software genuinely worth having is the customer relationship, based on mutual advantage and trust. Individual, differentiable customer relationships will be the ultimate software of businesses in the 1:1 future. All your products are ephemeral. Only your customers are real."

The internet not only accelerates many of the competitive threats to your products, but also can make many of your dealings with your customers or potential customers appear impersonal and lacking in human contact. So how can we use the benefits of the internet whilst at the same time creating and maintaining personal relationships?

There are many ways to develop relationships online. Email is probably the most widely used. Email your customers regular newsletters, advance notices, special offers, personalised news or links and articles that you think might be of interest to them. There are also software programs that allow you to personalise email (eg www.digital-impact.com, www.guesttrack.com).

However, where many companies fall down is in not having an email response policy. Many of today's internet users expect very prompt responses to email. Too many companies lose their chance to create a relationship by being slow or not responding to email messages. In a recent survey of 325 British web sites only 62% responded to a simple email query (see results at www.buchanan.co.uk). This means that 38% did not respond at all!

TIP

If you are not prepared to treat email seriously then it is better not to provide an email address

One leading Australian car insurance company took seven days to respond to a request for a car insurance quote. It would have been better if this company would not accept email quote requests but simply gave a telephone number. If you are not prepared to treat email seriously then it is better not to provide an email address.

If you do provide an email address then determine who is to answer them (including back ups for when the nominated person is away), in what time frame they are to be answered, and if appropriate, how responses are to be authorised. Companies can consider having autoresponders to acknowledge all queries, standard responses to frequently asked questions, and even work flow processes that notify senior managers if a response has not been sent within the agreed time frame.

Larger companies should consider email response software agents which can greatly automate email responses (examples can be found at www.brightware.com, www.mustang.com, www.mcsdallas.com (Calypso) and www.aditi.com (Talisma)).

Relationships can also be built and maintained by the use of chat rooms. An expert hosted chat forum can be quite a good way to drive traffic to your site provided it is properly marketed.

Discussion groups can not only create and maintain relationships between you and your customers, but also help customers get in touch with each other. These can be unmoderated in which case they have more credibility, or moderated if you prefer more control.

Discussion groups can be self hosted or you can utilise the increasingly powerful services provided by the free communities at www.dejanews.com or clubs at www.yahoo.com.

To create an on-line community can be an extremely powerful marketing tool. Arthur Armstrong and John Hagel in their book "Net Gain" divide these communities into four categories (which can overlap):

- Fantasy – where people take on different personalities or create new environments such as combining players from different sports teams to form "fantasy teams" which compete against other "fantasy teams".

- Relationship – where people who have shared life experiences (such as diseases) come together, mainly to support each other.

- Interest – where people with a common interest in a topic gather to learn and share about the topic.

- Transaction – where people buy and sell products and services.

If you are not going to create an on-line community (ie it may be too expensive or not appropriate) then you may want to consider existing communities which you can sponsor or place advertisements or advertorial on to draw customers to your site.

To deepen a relationship with a customer you need to find out more about their wants and needs. Therefore, make it easy for your customers to contact you. Make your email address prominent and easy to find, together with your toll free number. You can consider the use of forms to gather the required information, and customer surveys either on your site or emailed to your customers.

TIP

Make your email address prominent and easy to find, together with your toll free number

Also make it easy for customers to complain. When someone complains they are presenting you with an opportunity to collaborate in solving a problem. You can then build loyalty and referrals. Just make sure you have a good process for handling complaints with some agreed service levels so you can monitor your performance. Consider a prize or some reward for the best feedback or suggestion.

Relationships can also be built simply by getting people to repeatedly return to your web site. Gaining share of their desktop is a good way to gain top of mind awareness and hence sales. To get people to keep coming to your site you must provide them with a reason. This is often relevant, frequently changing information, especially if it can be personalised.

Personalisation can vary from having good navigation allowing people to easily find what they want, password protected private areas, cookies to allow the site to remember the user on repeat visits, personalised start pages (similar to many portals), databases producing personalised content on the fly, different entry pages for separate categories of users, or personalisation software (eg www.firefly.com, www.broadvision.com, www.guesttrack.com) for larger companies.

In the digital world there are now customers who have a better relationship with on-line companies with whom they have no human contact rather than bricks and mortar companies with whom they have a great deal of human contact. This is because they feel more in control of the relationship with the on-line company where they can get the information they want, when they want, rather than relying on some under-trained, under-resourced human sales person in an offline store.

With new technology (such as making a phone call direct from a web site), even people who want human contact with an on-line organisation will shortly be able to achieve that as well.

So while there is a danger that human relationships can be neglected on the internet, this does not have to be the case. In fact, if you are clever you can even provide as good, and for some people, better customer service online. So the challenge for all of us is to use the internet to enhance our customer relationships.

Rod Brooks is a senior consultant with Australian Business Advisers, a Victorian-based consultancy. http://www.abaconsulting.com.au

How to Make the Most of Email Press Releases

By Eric Ward

The rise of email as a legitimate and accepted form of corporate public relations has created new opportunities for transmitting press releases. But marketers need to know the rules for making best use of this resource, or risk wasting it altogether.

An email press release has some subtle but crucial differences from its traditional paper counterpart. A badly formed and formatted email press release can often mean the recipient hits the delete key before even attempting to read it. Too often, companies simply take the release they originally created for paper distribution, cut and paste it into an email message, and let it fly. This is a wasted opportunity. Here are some tips for making an email press release as effective as possible.

1) Never Spam

First and foremost, never spam or send untargeted mass mailings of any type. Automated PR is an oxymoron. Think about it, know your audience and respect them. Don't be too friendly, nor too formal.

Second, recognise that you need to make your release as reader-friendly as possible. A great number of email software packages exist, and each recipient may have a different one.

Some email packages let users change the font my email is displayed in, as well as the font I compose in. That's great if you have bad eyes, but this also means that a press release I read in each of these email programs looks remarkably different, and probably different from how it looked to the person who composed it.

2) Use Standard Font

To help bring consistency to your releases compose them in the standard Courier typeface in 10-point size. Then, type only 60 to 68 characters per line, hitting the return key to begin each and every new line.

Not hitting the return key can result in a "runaway line" that goes beyond the right margin of your email. This is common for users of Pine and Unix mail, which won't always automatically wrap your text.

You might also include a line of text in parentheses advising recipients to set the font of their email software to Courier 10 point for best reading. This is a common fixed-width font and is what most folks use when they create a release.

Third, include the right type of contact information. Usually, a press release has a contact person and phone number for more information. In an email press release, you need to also include the email address for the contact person and the URL for the company website.

3) Include The Url

Include the URL in a prominent location, also on its own line. I once received an email press release that went on and on about a new website, but they forgot to include the URL. Another had the URL in a long line of text that made it tricky for me to cut and paste in my web browser.

Both of these fairly minor formatting points left me frustrated with these releases, and I never did visit the websites themselves.

Now imagine you are an editor or reporter who receives 50 such press releases a day, most of them badly formatted and not user-friendly. It becomes easy to see why the delete button gets heavy use.

4) Be Descriptive in Intro

Finally, use a descriptive subject line in your email. This is the first thing most of us see when we open our mail, and more often than not to choose which email I read by the content in the subject line.

Don't simply type "Press Release" on your subject line. Check the sample subject lines below, and see which one you'd be more inclined to read. An example is: Subject: ACME to Launch RoadRunner Server v2.0 Monday

Some might argue that by telling too much in the subject, you risk having editors delete it. But the editors who don't want your news release won't be fooled either way, and this way it will reach the ones who do need it.

Eric Ward is the founder of website awareness-building services NetPOST and URLwire and is a former marketing director at Whittle Communications. He can be reached at ericward@urlwire.com

How to Measure Email Marketing Campaigns

By Lia Timson

N ew technologies bring with them new practices and with those new standards are slowly being established. In email marketing these standards are yet to be set in stone as are consumers yet to determine what is and is not effective on them.

This includes trustworthy measurement techniques for email marketing effectiveness, or, for that matter, any internet marketing effort. "Anyone who says they can forecast response rates (in direct email) is lying to you," says Malcolm Auld, one of Australia's leading direct marketing specialists and executive director of Thompson Connect, the direct mail arm of advertising agency J. Walter Thompson.

"All they can do is send an offer to a list and expect a similar response rate if they send another offer to that same list." Traditional direct mailing techniques call for an average two to three percent response rate when a list is rented and there is no established relationship with the recipients.

The same may not apply to email marketing where the addressee is known to the marketer by way of previous registration or account holding. "It is far too early to say what internet marketing even is," says Scott McClellan, communications director of the Australian Direct Marketing Association (ADMA).

He says companies have experienced minimal response rates thus far because the few campaigns undertaken to-date have been untargeted. "A CD-Rom may have 25 million addresses on it. That is not direct marketing, it's abuse of the marketing medium, annoyance really," he says.

According to Auld, some campaigns to lists known to the sender and welcome by the recipient by way of permission to be contacted, have yielded up to 15% response rate. "But you can potentially get 80 to 90% response if you know the customer," Auld says.

Yahoo's advertising sales director, Craig Lambert, says responses can really only be measured through click-through rates indicating the recipient was at least tempted to know more about the offer advertised. "They can click through and act on the offer straight away. The response time is extremely rapid. Within a week you can launch, market and get a response," he says.

Yahoo's new Y!Delivers program is now selling Yahoo customer e-mail addresses to marketers at a rate of $0.75 per address plus $0.25 per filter such as sex and age. These are addresses obtained through the opt-in system which Lambert says is a reliable source of consumers who are willing to receive information.

But Auld says the impact of the message on brands has not yet been measured by any established methodologies. "Traditional research companies that track brand values for television, radio and press campaigns, don't yet do it for email marketing, not even for direct marketing," he says.

This means the standard of your email list and the strength of both your relationship with the addressee and the strength of your offer are crucial to the rate of your email marketing success.

Auld says any request for the recipient to part with money must include a meaningful offer. However, if the communication is simply a meaningful dialogue between established supplier and customer, offers can be omitted. This applies, for example, to a market survey for improved customer service. "The dialogue is a lot quicker, because the message is already open in front of you," he says suggesting recipients are more compelled to respond and deal with the item, than they would through traditional mail.

By late October, the Australian market may know a little more about this practice. Yahoo! is planning on making public the results of its first Y!Delivers pilot with internet gift supplier wishlist.com.au.

The strength of the responses will propel Yahoo! to clinch deals with larger brands eager to establish a dialogue with consumers ready to receive offers. In which case the key will be whether those customers allowing the use of their email addresses are really conscious of the extent of their permission.

Lia Timson is a Sydney-based freelance journalist and regular contributor to E-Commerce Today. http://www.ecommercetoday.com.au

The Benefits of Targeted Opt-in Email Marketing

Email direct marketing campaigns in the US — opt-in based campaigns that is — are yielding above average results, depending on how targeted the list is. Even though opt-in email marketing has been around for just two years, 70% of companies interviewed by US-based research firm Forrester Research saw it as "important" or "very important" (see figure 1-1).

Most of the 50 online retailers, manufacturers and media companies that Forrester interviewed for the report in March this year used opt-in email lists for product promotions and newsletters. Interviewees reported getting click-through rates of 14-22%. The conversion rates to sales was around 4%. This compares to the 1-2% traditional print (usually unsolicited) direct mail generates.

The response rate is even better than the sometimes maligned website banner advertising. The click-through rates for banner advertising generates an average of 0.65%, according to Forrester, whereas opt-in targeted email delivers a "dreamlike" 18% on average.

The other lure is that it is cheaper, much cheaper. There are draw-backs. It requires technology and email management. Many marketers still use their own in-house systems — often using Eudora or Microsoft Outlook or other standard programs.

"As outbound email evolves from spam to direct marketing to a central point of contact, firms must acquire news competencies and technology to retain the customers that they fought so hard to attract," Forrester concludes. It says there are three "imperatives" for successful email marketing: personally delivered content; user-centred design and; anytime, anywhere delivery.

To the question "How Important is Email to Your Sales and Marketing Strategy" the responses were as follows:

Very important	38%
Important	32%
Unimportant	24%
Very unimportant	6%

SOURCE: Forrester Research Inc, 1999 ©.

To the question "What Are Your Using Outbound Email For?"
the responses were as follows:

Promotions and discounts	66%
Newsletter	48%
Product releases	34%
Advertising/marketing	28%
Alerts/reminders	24%
Market research	8%
Other	4%

SOURCE: Forrester Research Inc, 1999 ©.

Email Formatting – html or Text?

Email can be sent in html (hypertext markup language) formatting, like a website, as well as plain text. The attraction of sending html email is the enhanced appearance. You can include pictures, logos, colour, anything, to make your email more beautiful.

Some of the problems of sending html email include:

- It can alienate your customers who are not as technologically up to date as you;

- It can also frustrate email recipients when there are compatibility problems between email programs that can access html;

- Downloading time can discourage viewing your email; and

- Customers may have to be online to access certain html features like hyperlinks and graphics, and as such, your email can cost them money.

New-York based online marketing firm, MMG, wanted to investigate which format works best: whether people were ready for dynamic, graphically enhanced messages, or was the simplicity of straight text one of email's greatest strengths? The company conducted an online survey of users of one of its discussion lists in January 1999 to find out.

The survey's goal was to gather quantitative data in addition to the qualitative input provided by posts to the discussion list. Participants could vote for html, text, or indifferent, and receive an immediate cumulative total of all votes. The results favoured plain text:

Email Preference	Percent	Number
Text	63%	772
html	24%	297
Depends on publication	8%	101
Indifferent	5%	57
Total	100%	1227

Text vs html

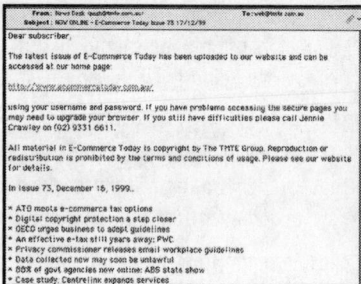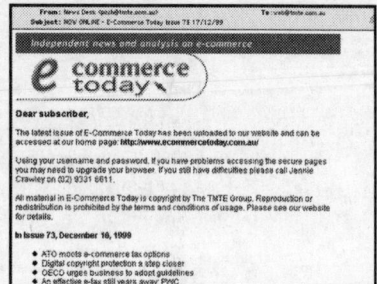

Customers are Resisting html Email

Around one third of US marketers use html email but, despite this, many believe it has serious failings, according to US-based research company Forrester Research.

It conducted a survey of online retailers, manufacturers and media companies that use opt-in email and found that low penetration of html-enabled email recipients or customers are key obstacles to it taking over from text-based email.

However, it also found that click-through [to website] rates doubled and that html emails generated better user experiences. It concluded that, despite resistance from the customer side, companies plan to use more of it in the future.

In fact, it predicted that service providers like AOL would, before long, html-enable its own email client technology for customers and that, within two years, browser and email client functionality would merge "making messages indistinguishable from web pages".

To the question "Are You Using html Email?"
the responses were as follows:

Yes	34%
No	66%
Yes, plan to use it two years	64%
No, don't plan to use it in two years	10%

SOURCE: Forrester Research Inc, 1999 ©.

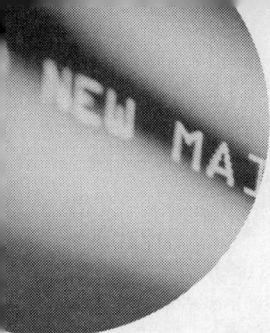

Email Broadcasting Uncovered – Nine Things You Need to Know

By Tim O'Connor

Email broadcasting, or direct email as it's sometimes called, is definitely the hot new marketing tool. You've probably received at least a few commercial email messages yourself in the past few months. How did you respond to them? If the messages you received were unsolicited, you likely discarded them or unsubscribed immediately, while mentally decrying the unwelcome intrusion.

If they arrived from organisations who first asked your permission to send you information via email, you probably felt much better about their arrival in your inbox and took a moment to peruse the contents. You may have even discovered a great offer on a product you'd been wanting to buy.

Herein lies the great divide in the world of email marketing:

The dreaded "spammers" vs. the responsible email marketers. Fortunately, the latter group has greatly improved the image email broadcasting over the past year by developing best practices for this medium. Customers are quickly learning by experience not all commercial email is bad — in fact it can deliver great value and convenience when used effectively.

The hype associated with email marketing is not unjustified. The medium has a lot going for it: low cost of entry, quick turnaround, great interactive potential, double-digit response rates, high per-campaign ROI.

Nine things you need to know to email broadcast properly follow on the next page.

1) Grow Your Own List

While many list brokers will gladly sell you lists of "targeted email addresses", this is not the way to generate high response rates and build good customer relationships via email. Instead make the effort to grow your email address database in-house. Start by gathering email addresses on all your print and digital media order forms, response cards, website etc.

Whenever possible, gather relevant information (company, title, topics of interest, etc) at the same time so that you can target your subsequent email campaigns appropriately. When asking for an email address, it's a good idea to indicate that the address will be used for email communications.

2) Use a Straightforward, Descriptive Subject Line

Tests of response rates have shown that the KISS principle applies to email broadcasting too. Don't try to entice the recipient into opening your email message with a mysterious or cute subject line. Instead, include a subject line that paraphrases the body of the message with concise, straightforward language.

3) Mention Why You're Contacting the Recipient

To start off on the right note, include a very brief explanation of your reason for contacting the recipient via email at the top of your message. Perhaps the individual signed up for your mailing list at a trade show or subscribed to your monthly newsletter on your web site. The best email etiquette requires that you gently remind the recipient that they did indeed initiate your email dialogue.

4) Keep it Short and Sweet

Put yourself in the shoes of your audience. Would you want to read a long email message just to understand what the sender is offering you? Deliver the value high up in the message and give readers the option to click on embedded links or call a toll-free number to get to more information or place an order.

5) Personalise Each Email

As with other types of direct marketing, personalisation will increase the impact of your message. At minimum, consider personalising your message with the recipient's first name; you may want to merge other database information into the body of your message that will tailor it even further.

6) Include a Call to Action

This may sound like a no-brainer, but it's one you don't want to forget! In designing your email campaign, come up with a call to action that suits the offer and the audience. It could be a toll-free number or an embedded URL that links to a special promotion on your website.

7) Give the Recipient the Option to Unsubscribe

At this point in its short history, there are few regulations policing the sending of commercial email messages. However, there's one you need to heed: include a link at the bottom of your message that invites the recipient to "unsubscribe" (also called "opting out") from future email communications. If your company sends a variety of email communications (newsletter, technical tips, channel/reseller news, product line updates, etc.), you may want to build a web page where your customers can pick and choose from a list of email communications in one central location.

8) Remember, the Trick is in the Receiving not the Sending

There's no great magic involved in sending out high volumes of email messages. This isn't where an email broadcasting vendor can offer you much value. The tricky part is managing the bounce-backs and responses that come pouring in after the broadcast has gone out to maintain the quality of your future email communications. You'll want to track responses. Flag unsubscribe requests and handle responder comments/questions efficiently. And correct bad addresses.

9) Monitor the Frequency of Email Communications

It's very important that you track how frequently your company is sending emails to individual recipients to avoid over-saturation. The low cost and quick turnaround associated with email broadcasting can translate into unintended abuse if multiple departments within your company are using your email database. There are many good reasons to send email – product updates, technical tips, promotions, order confirmations – but, as always, timing is everything.

Tim O'Connor is an account executive with Epigraphx, an electronic communications services company based in Redmond City, California, US, whose services include email broadcasting. http://www.epigraphx.com/

Fast Facts

Sending of solicited commercial email (SCE) is quickly gaining in popularity among marketers. Forrester Research projects that 250 billion SCE messages will be sent by 2002.

263 million email boxes now exist worldwide, according to the newsletter "Electronic Mail Messaging Systems".

A survey of 60 leading marketers by New York-based Gruppo, Levey & Co found that 40%, of the marketers currently conduct email direct campaigns, while another 37% plan to do so in the near future.

Top 10 Permission Marketing Tips from Yahoo! Australia & NZ

1) Permission marketing needs to be anticipated – so that people look forward to hearing from you

2) Permission marketing needs to be personal – with the message directly related to the individual

3) Permission marketing needs to be relevant – the marketing has to be about something the prospect is interested in

4) Permission marketing requires patience, because it takes time to turn strangers into friends, and friends into customers

5) You need to offer the prospect an incentive to volunteer information and/or permission

6) Over time, you can use the customer's permission to teach the consumer about your product/service

7) You then need to then reinforce the incentive/offer new ones to guarantee that the prospect maintains the permission over time

8) The customer can cancel permission at any time if you abuse their trust

9) As advertising clutter increases, permission is worth more and is harder to get. In every market segment, only a limited number of companies will be able to secure permission

10) Nothing great is free, and that goes double for permission. Acquiring solid, deep permission from targeted customers is an investment.

These tips were developed by Yahoo! with help from Seth Godin. Yahoo! has a page of information about spamming at http://help.yahoo.com/help/au/mail/spam/

Spam, Scams and Shams

Introduction

S pam, Scams, Unsolicited Bulk Email, Unsolicited Commercial Email and Junk Email – unwanted nuisance email – is the most hotly debated issue relating to email use.

Any internet search using the term "spam" will result in countless matches, offering spammer-blacklists, national and international anti-spam lobby groups, advice and software for blocking and filtering spam, discussion groups, reporting services, spam hunters, spam cops, spam wars and so on.

What Is Spam?

Put simply, spam is unwanted email.

There are variations on definitions and titles: Spam, Unsolicited Bulk Email (UBE), Unsolicited Commercial Email (UCE) and Junk Email. And there are also spoof and email scams. This chapter covers all of these topics.

Most spam is unsolicited and is usually part of a bulk commercial emailing campaign to sell goods and services that the recipient does not want.

Sometimes a person asks for information once or wants to receive email messages from one particular organisation only – but their email address is then added or sold to another mailing list. They can then be on the receiving end of copious spam messages. Once on such a list it can be nearly impossible to be removed.

A detailed discussion of the definitions of spam is addressed in an article: "Why Spam is Bad?" later in this chapter. Then a selection of spam categories "Spam at a Glance" provides a snapshot of spam content for those who have somehow avoided receiving nuisance email and who want to know more.

Of course, there are some individuals out there who actually like spam, but they are a small, silent minority. For most email users, spam is public enemy number one. Judging by the time, web-space and passion invested in the topic, it is the email we love to hate.

Why Is Spam So Reviled?

The main reasons spam is so reviled include the time it wastes and the drain it has on computer networks. In "Spam - The Productivity Killer" in this chapter it is argued there is "no more efficient means of consuming the time, money and resources of millions against their will" than spam.

In "Time Is Money — The Cost Of Unwanted Email", Paul Hoffman discusses the real and social cost of unsolicited bulk email to the receiver and adds that, as well as causing lost productivity, UBE can also discourage using email to its fullest potential.

Spam Is Super-Junk Mail

The fact that spam does not waste paper like the junk mail you get in your letterbox at home is probably its greatest defence. But it is because of this very accessibility, made possible without printing and physical distribution costs, that spam has been able to take off on a truly global scale, allowing literally anyone to send out enormous amounts of junk mail to innumerable recipients. And they do.

What To Do About Spam?

A huge legion of anti-spam warriors exists on the internet who are ready to offer assistance with spam management. Another good place to get started is the list of anti-spam resources in the URL Guide at the end of this chapter.

The "How to Block Spam" article covers the pros and cons of different spam filtering techniques and also addresses the related issues of spoof and relay. Methods of reporting and blocking spam, as well as a step-by-step guide to tracking spam, are demonstrated later.

Can Spam Be Outlawed?

There is strong pressure for both the self-regulation of commercial email practices and for government intervention. The Australian Direct Marketing Association (ADMA) recommends in this chapter the use of world best practice, as determined by the Organisation for Economic Cooperation and Development (OECD) and an individual focus by Internet Service Providers (ISPs) in monitoring and punishing spammers.

As spam can be, and often is, used for scams and illegal methods of fundraising, this chapter includes advice from the Australian Securities and Investments Commission on identifying and avoiding email scams. Also, a case study of a recent international spam rip-off, the "FreeBan" internet share scam, shows how spam is used in unethical business practices and to increase the pool of potential spam recipients.

Spam Doesn't Work

The paradox of spam is that, despite its ubiquity, it is a failure as a marketing ploy. It just doesn't have anywhere near the same success as other direct marketing strategies such as opt-in permission marketing which is discussed in more detail in the marketing chapters.

The dangers presented by spam to business are not just incoming messages. As spam is considered the ultimate email etiquette no-no, your business cannot afford to be labelled a spammer.

Why Spam is Bad

By Barry Saiff

Have you ever received an email message from a website you visited, but could not remember whether or not you agreed to be on the mailing list? Some people say you cannot have one definition of spam for everyone. I propose here a simple definition of spam that I think makes this kind of "spam is in the eyes of the beholder" approach unnecessary. See if you agree.

Spam is unsolicited email. "Unsolicited" means the recipient of the email message did not request to receive the message. It is not always possible to directly determine if an email message is unsolicited. This is true even for the end user. In the example above, recipients would not know for sure if the email was solicited or unsolicited. On the other hand, consider these cases:

- You receive an email from an unknown source because when you visited a website or participated in a chat room, your email address was "harvested" and added to a list of addresses used by spammers.

- Your address was added to a spammer's address list through other means, without your knowledge.

- You agreed to receive email when you signed up for a service on the internet.

Each of these cases is different from the perspective of defining spam. How do you distinguish which of these messages is spam and which is not? Remember, the key word here is unsolicited.

There are several factors, often used to define spam, which are useful as indicators or "clues" to the solicited or unsolicited nature of an email message.

Removal Option

The most important clue is a removal option.

- Does the email message provide a method for the user to "opt out" from receiving any further emails?

- When used, does this removal option work or just lead to more unsolicited email messages?

- Some less legitimate senders of email actually sell removal response messages to other companies who send further unsolicited emails to these "confirmed live" email accounts. However, the presence of an effective removal option in the email message does not by itself mean the message is not spam. If the message was unsolicited, it is still spam.

Bulk Commercial Email

TIP

The most important clue is a "removal option"

Another important clue is whether the email message is BULK email. In other words, were multiple copies of this email message sent? In most cases, you as the user cannot tell, as you receive only one copy and cannot know if one or one million such messages were sent. In some cases you yourself receive multiple copies of the same message. This clue alone does not identify a message as spam, as many legitimate, solicited email messages are sent in bulk. Any of a multitude of "opt-in" lists are used to distribute these messages. For example, American Express, Amazon.com and many other "A" companies send regular emails to customers who have requested to receive them. ("B" through "Z" companies have also been known to do this!)

Relationship Between Sender and Recipient

A third clue to the unsolicited nature of an email message is the lack of any prior relationship between sender and recipient. If you receive email from a person or company that you never heard of, it is unlikely that you requested to receive the email. However, you can also receive unsolicited email messages from companies and individuals with whom you do already have relationships.

Content of the Email

Finally, the content of an email may provide clues as to whether it was unsolicited. Does the content of the email message:

- Advertise something for sale

- Offer money-making opportunities

- Advertise pornographic websites or products

- Contain offensive material

- Otherwise follow patterns typical of many other already-identified spam messages

- Contain or attach dangerous software code?

Many of these common types of email, such as Make Money Fast (MMF) and Multi-Level Marketing (MLM) messages, are often less than fully legal attempts to involve consumers in schemes that may be completely fraudulent.

- On the internet, as elsewhere, dealing with an organisation that you know has an interest in maintaining their good name is one way to avoid being the victim of a crime.

- Certain patterns are often followed by senders of spam, but not consistently. For example, does the text include liberal amounts of ALL CAPS and multiple exclamation (!!!) points?

- Any of these patterns by itself could be followed by a legitimate message, so this clue alone is not sufficient to define spam.

Conclusion

The clues discussed here are some of those used by the Brightmail Anti-Spam Service to determine whether a message is spam. If Brightmail, Inc. could ask each user whether they had requested the email, we would not need to use these indirect clues. Because it is not practical to do that for each message, we use a combination of clues to judge whether a specific email message is unsolicited.

No single clue alone causes Brightmail to treat a piece of email as spam.

Barry Saiff is from Brightmail http://www.brightmail.com

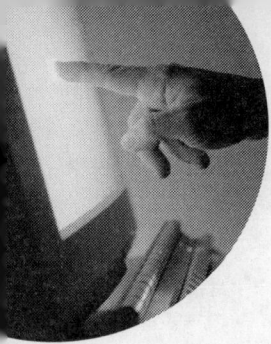

An Examination of What is in Spam?

I n Brightmail's attempt to learn more about spam and its effect on business, the company has collected spam samples and divided them into the following categories:

1) Business Opportunity Scams

Most of these scams promise a lot of income for a small investment of time and money. Some are actually old-fashioned pyramid schemes camouflaged to look like something else.

2) Making Money by Sending Bulk Email

These spams actually offer email address lists or software to allow you to become a spammer! What they don't tell you is that the lists are of poor quality, that sending bulk email violates most ISPs' terms of service, that virtually no legitimate businesses engage in bulk emailings and that several US states have laws regulating the transmission of bulk email.

3) Chain Letters

These electronic versions of old-fashioned chain letters usually arrive with claims such as: "You can make $50,000 in less than 90 days!"

4) Work-at-Home Schemes

These messages offer the chance to earn money in the comfort of your own home. Two popular versions pitch envelope stuffing and craft assembly. But nobody will really pay you for stuffing envelopes and craft assembly promoters usually refuse to buy the crafts, claiming the work does not meet their "quality standards".

5) Health and Diet Scams

These spams offer "scientific breakthroughs", "miraculous cures", "secret formulas", and "ancient ingredients". Some come with testimonials from "cured" consumers or endorsements from "famous medical experts" who no one's ever heard of.

6) Get-Rich-Quick

These offers, such as: "Learn how to make $4,000 in one day", or "Make unlimited profits exchanging money on world currency markets", appeal to everyone's desire to make money without working.

7) Get Something Free

The idea of getting valuable items for free lures consumers into paying membership fees to sign up with these scams. After they pay the fee, consumers learn they don't qualify for the "free" gift until they recruit other "members".

8) Investment Opportunities

These scams usually tout unrealistically high rates of return with no risk. Glib promoters suggest they have high-level financial connections, inside information or guaranteed investments. They may offer phony statistics, misrepresent the significance of a current event or stress the unique quality of their offer.

9) Cable De-Scrambler Kits

For a small initial investment you can buy a cable descrambler kit so you can receive cable without paying the subscription fees.

10) Guaranteed Loans or Credit on Easy Terms

Some offer home-equity loans, even if you don't have any equity in your home. Others offer guaranteed, unsecured credit cards, regardless of your credit history. The "loans" turn out to be lists of lending institutions and the credit cards never arrive.

11) Credit Repair Scams

These scams target consumers with poor credit records. For an up-front fee, they offer to clear up a bad credit record -- for a fee.

12) Vacation Prize Promotions

Like their snail mail counterparts, these email "Prize Promotions" tell consumers they've been selected to receive a "luxury" vacation at a bargain-basement price. But the accommodation isn't deluxe and upgrades are expensive.

13) Pornographic Spam

Children are the primary victims of sexually-oriented spam. An AT&T study determined that 11 percent of spam is adult-themed content

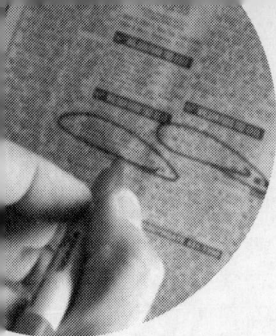

What Does Spam Advertise?

By Lorrie Faith Cranor and Brian A. LaMacchia

As part of a study on spam, a collection of 400 unique messages sent to the AT&T and Lucent sub-domains during March, April, and May 1997 were identified by email administrators as spam and then analysed.

Thirty-six percent of the messages in the collection advertised money-making opportunities, including pyramid-style schemes, multi-level marketing systems, and investment opportunities.

Eleven percent advertised adult entertainment, singles services, and sexually-oriented products and services. Ten percent advertised direct email marketing products and services, including bulk email services, lists of email addresses, and software for harvesting email addresses or sending out bulk mailings. Nine percent advertised informational and how-to guides.

Seven percent advertised internet services and various computer hardware and software products, office supplies and machinery, and related services. Three percent were either non-commercial messages or suspected to have been solicited by the recipient. The remaining messages advertised other products and services, including phone services, vacation packages, nutritional supplements, weight loss products, credit cards, cable descramblers, and online newsletters.

Only 36% of the messages contained instructions for being removed from the mailing list — and reports from email administrators suggest many of these instructions are likely faulty or deliberately misleading. Perhaps most telling about the nature of these messages was the fact that fewer than 10% identified the name, postal address, phone number, and email address of the sender, as per the Direct Marketing Association (DMA) guidelines (see http://www.the-dma.org/home_pages/business-affairs/onlinebd.html).

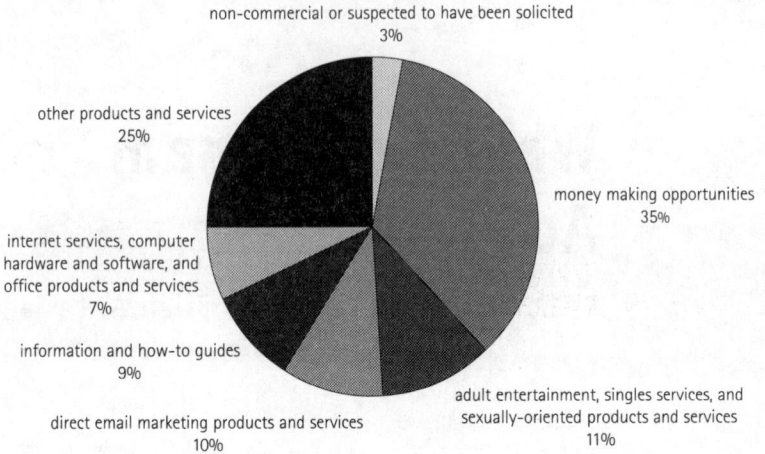

non-commercial or suspected to have been solicited
3%

other products and services
25%

money making opportunities
35%

internet services, computer hardware and software, and office products and services
7%

information and how-to guides
9%

direct email marketing products and services
10%

adult entertainment, singles services, and sexually-oriented products and services
11%

The low percentage of identified senders and observations about the types of products and services being offered support the general perception among spam recipients that most spam is not coming from "legitimate businesses". Indeed spam recipients often complain that spam is particularly annoying to them because so much of it advertises adult entertainment and possibly-fraudulent schemes.

When H. Robert Weintzen, president of the DMA, spoke at the June 1997 FTC workshop about spam he said, "Most legitimate marketers are afraid to be associated with it". Others at the workshop expressed concern that a fear of spam would deter people from engaging in electronic commerce.

This is an excerpt from research "Types of Products and Services Advertised in Analysed Spam Samples". Reprinted with permission from the Association of Computing Machinery. http://www.acm.org

Lorrie Faith Cranor is from AT&T and Brian A. LaMacchia is from Microsoft.

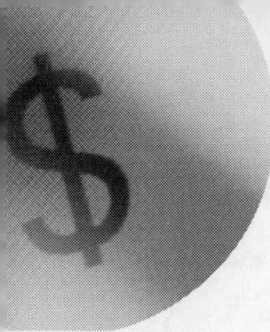

Time is Money – The Cost of Unwanted Email

By Paul Hoffman

U nsolicited Bulk Email UBE has become a major concern for internet users, due to the increasing amount of UBE that typical internet users receive. Many proposals for technical and legislative remedies are being suggested, but few proposals define UBE or list its negative effects. This article sets forth standard definitions and gives an overview of UBE effects, without proposing or supporting particular mechanisms for controlling their occurrence.

Unsolicited Bulk Email

Unsolicited Bulk Email, or UBE, is internet mail ("email") sent to a group of recipients who have not requested it. A mail recipient may have at one time asked a sender for bulk email, but then later asked that sender not to send any more email or otherwise not have indicated a desire for additional mail, so any bulk email sent after the request was received also constitutes UBE.

A common term for UBE is "spam", although that term encompasses a wider range of intrusive transmissions. For instance, the term "spam" originated in the realm of Usenet news, not email. There, individuals cannot request or refuse bulk email, although some newsgroups explicitly permit or encourage its inclusion as a part of the group charter.

Note: the first version of this report used the term Unsolicited Commercial Email. That term was originally chosen because much of the early debate about UBE was centred in the United States where commercial speech can be regulated by the government but political and religious speech cannot. However, on reflection, because UBE is an international problem, the term "UCE" was changed in this report to "UBE". Limitations on the control of UBE, such as having to have different laws for political UBE versus commercial UBE, is a local matter.

Problems Caused By UBE

Although the senders of UBE defend it as having little difference from traditional bulk mail, in fact it is quite different: UBE shifts almost all the costs of the message onto email recipients and their destination operators (See article about The Role of ISP's and Destination Operators).

Many senders of UBE use tactics which are often viewed as devious and are probably illegal, in order to reduce the cost to the sender or even hide the true identity of the sender. Instead, costs are shifted from the sender to the receiver.

Effects On Recipients

A recipient is a person who receives email. Most recipients usually receive email from two kinds of senders - other people and Mailing List Agents. Some email addresses refer to a "role" within the organisation (such as "sales" or "postmaster") and might have multiple people processing email or a software program responding automatically. In either case, UBE must still be handled by the recipient.

End users are the ones who are most affected by UBE. The costs to recipients generally fall into two categories: real costs and social costs.

Real Costs

UBE costs money to every recipient, as if it was sent "postage due". Probably the most important negative effect of UBE is the financial cost incurred in transmitting it to the recipient, such as through a modem. Many users have to pay internet access providers by the minute. Even users with fixed-cost internet accounts often have to pay for phone time to connect to internet access providers. Multiply these costs by the hundreds of thousands or millions of users that many pieces of UBE go to and you can see that the cost to recipients is quite high.

There are other costs paid by all UBE recipients that are similar to recipients of bulk postal mail.

For instance there is the time lost sorting UBE from wanted mail, the time lost opening unwanted UBE that is disguised as email that the user might want to read and so on. As the quantity of UBE increases, the cost of doing this sorting can become quite significant. UBE is a particular issue for companies where employees get email, since dealing with UBE is done on company time, thus causing lost productivity.

Social and Personal Costs

Widespread UBE has had a significant human cost as well. Many users know that posting to mailing lists or on Usenet news will likely cause them to receive UBE, so they no longer participate in what used to be the most vibrant communications medium on the internet.

The constant fear of irreversibly getting one's name on a mailing list has caused many people to avoid using them altogether. Similarly, the act of having to sort through cleverly-worded UBE in order to find actual personal email has caused many people not to use email to its fullest potential.

These types of effects are causing many new users to avoid checking their mail as often as they would otherwise like, again causing less use of what could be a valuable medium. The use of "filters" by a recipient's email software can reduce some of this pain, but cannot eliminate it. The current state of filtering technology cannot distinguish between legitimate, personal email and UBE.

Paul Hoffman is from Internet Mail Consortium, an industry trade association for companies participating in the internet mail market. You can get the newest version of this report in full from the IMC website http://www.imc.org/ube-def.html

Spam – The Office Productivity Killer

Some companies have publicly estimated that upwards of 30% of their daily email traffic is spam, which is also known as junk email. According to an online survey by World Research, 40% of respondents receive "heavy to very heavy" amounts of junk email every day. In fact, according to recent US Senate testimony from the Coalition Against Unsolicited Commercial Email (CAUCE), a few days of junk email for an ISP the size of AOL would fill the disk storage space of every office computer on Capitol Hill.

"There is no other medium quite like junk email in its ability to damage internet systems," testified CAUCE co-founder Ray Everett-Church. "I know of no more efficient means of consuming the time, money and resources of millions against their will." What does this flood of junk email mean for your business? A "spam jam" can hit the bottom line when business-critical messages are delayed.

Junk Email Not Useful

The productivity of workers is adversely affected by the volume of unsolicited email they must wade through every day. According to World Research, 70% of those surveyed report that "junk email was not useful at all".

It is up to your company to limit the amount of spam your employees receive. You cannot wait for your ISPs to control it, despite their many efforts to do so. CAUCE reports that junk email has "knocked out" systems belonging to major internet service providers such as AT&T, @Home, Pacific Bell, Netcomm and GTE.

One major network reports that despite developing software to block spam and doubling the number of its computers dedicated to controlling junk email, the incidence of spam has not fallen because the number of spammers — with new efforts to get around anti-spam strategies — counter these efforts at every turn.

"This is literally an arms race," says Darrel Baker, a senior system engineer with Concentric Networks, which operates in 50 US states and Canada. "We block spam and then junk emailers figure out a strategy to get around it. We implement a response to the strategy, and then they come up with something new."

ISPs Can't Control the Flow

Since ISPs may not be able to control the amount of spam your company receives by improving their technology, can they limit it by challenging a spammer's rights to use their networks? According to David Kramer, an attorney with Wilson Sonsni Goodrich and Rosati, who successfully represented Concentric Networks and CompuServe in litigation against the spammer Cyber Promotions, this is not usually a viable option, because the court-related costs of challenges are prohibitive.

"There are thousands of such companies and the number is growing," he explains. "I know of no small ISP that has been able to recoup damages commensurate with the impact on their business. If someone says we can recoup damages via the courts for such actions without new legislation, I would love to have their help in doing so."

But efforts to control spam legislatively are blocked by marketing advocates who believe the recipient — your company — should be responsible for deleting unwanted email — despite the fact that you bear the cost in clogged networks and lost productivity before you have the option to delete the message. While organisations such as CAUCE, the Internet Mail Consortium and the Internet Service Providers' Consortium support efforts to regulate spam, it is still open season for spammers.

According to David Sorkin of the John Marshall Law School: "The Federal Trade Commission says they want to wait for people to discuss private solutions — self-regulation by the (spamming) industry or technical solutions. I don't have much faith that self-regulation will do much to solve the problem and I expect the FTC does not as well, but they are going to give that some time."

As the debate on legislation continues, your company's productivity loss through spamming increases.

This article was provided by Content Technologies and is an excerpt from an article "Internet Liability: The New Legal Risk to Business", a white paper on content security. http://www.mimesweeper.com.au

The Role of ISPs and Destination Operators

By Paul Hoffman

Core problems associated with UBE stem from the very low cost on the sender and the real costs imposed on recipients and their destination operators. There is no other common form of unsolicited communication that shifts so much of the cost of each message onto the recipients. The costs are particularly high on novice users and the destination operators who have a preponderance of novice user clients, but the costs are in fact borne by all internet users.

What is a destination operator? Internet email is processed by origination, relay and destination system (host) operators, primarily transmitting messages with the SMTP mail standard.

An origination operator is an organisation or individual that is responsible for the host which places a new piece of email into the internet. A relay operator mediates email transmission between origination and destination systems.

A destination operator is an organisation or individual that maintains or controls a service for recipients of email and allows recipients to access their mail using a mail user agent. Destination operators may also provide relay services and almost always provide origination service for the same users who are recipients.

What is the difference between an internet service provider and a destination operator? These specialised terms are used here instead of the single, more common "internet service provider" because tens of millions of people get their mail service from organisations that are not ISPs.

Almost everyone who gets email at their desk at work uses their employers as a destination operator, but those companies are not ISPs. Also, many people get their internet mail through free accounts in public libraries, schools and so on, and the organisations running those mail servers should be differentiated from ISPs because they often offer email access as a public service.

In many cases, ISPs which provide basic connectivity have no direct part in the problems associated with UBE. On the other hand, all internet mail operators must deal with UBE problems every day.

The terms introduced here include organisations providing internet mail service to employees, as well as libraries and schools providing free service for their "customers" and also includes ISPs that include email within their set of products.

Effects Of UBE on Destination Operators

The costs of UBE go well beyond the recipient. Each destination operator pays for each email message received because a message takes up a certain amount of the destination operator's connectivity and computer bandwidth. Further, if the message is stored by the destination operator for a recipient, the operator must pay for the storage and the maintenance of that storage. Although the cost of a single UBE email to an individual recipient might well be quite small, the aggregate cost can be considerable.

How do destination operators handle the cost of UBE? Depending upon their specific business model, each destination operator handles the costs of UBE differently. If the destination operator is an internet service provider, the costs of UBE are borne by the ISP's users, through higher prices or lower service.

If the destination operator is an employer, the costs of UBE are often taken out of the general networking budget, meaning that UBE causes lower company profits. If the destination operator is someone offering a free public mail service, UBE causes them to be able to offer less service to their clients.

Many destination operators report that they bear an additional and considerable expense, one of having to educate people about the nature of UBE and why they are receiving it. Because UBE tends to diminish people's desire to use the internet, they are more likely to complain about it to their destination operators.

Effects On The Internet Backbone

UBE sent over the internet backbone causes delays for all internet users. Further, because most UBE senders use mailing lists that have outdated addresses on them, many messages are rejected ("bounced"), causing the intended destination operator to send a return response, which wastes more bandwidth.

Effects Caused By Malicious UBE Senders

Many of the complaints about UBE, by destination operators, stem from the common practice employed by UBE senders of misappropriating services. The methods of misappropriation, while technically easy to do, cause hundreds of thousands of dollars of damage to destination operators per year by shifting the burden of sending the UBE on destination operators who are unrelated to the UBE sender.

The typical way that a deceptive UBE sender misappropriates service is to offload return mail and complaint handling onto an unsuspecting origination or relay operator by specifying one or more incorrect return addresses in the message itself.

They route the UBE through an unrelated origination operator's SMTP service. Both of these actions are quite easy to do and can make the source of the message almost untraceable, particularly if the UBE sender is using a short-lived internet account that was obtained for the purpose of sending this UBE. The account is used once, to do the sending, and is never accessed again. Hence, the sender need not care at all whether its use for this purpose is ascertained.

Beyond the basic cost of deceptive use, the result of the unwanted mailing often causes many complaints to be directed at the destination operator that should instead have been directed at the UBE sender. These complaints can cause significant damage to the destination operator such as by filling up mailboxes on the mail hosts and reducing service to legitimate users of the destination operator.

Paul Hoffman is from Internet Mail Consortium, an industry trade association for companies participating in the internet mail market.
http://www.imc.org/ube-def.html

How to Block Spam

By Andy Harris

D ealing with spam and spoof is not straightforward. There are a multitude of problems to be dealt with on a number of levels. Crude spam control will block business email and just because IP address and domains don't tie up, it is not necessarily spoof email. With effective anti-relay control, organsations can ensure they are not used as launching pads for spam or are spoofed from their own systems.

Users get on spammers' mailing lists by several routes. The most common is posting a reply to a newsgroup. Spammers have automated programs that crawl through newsgroups harvesting anything that looks like a valid email address. Another common route is by subscribing to mail lists or filling in forms on websites.

Using a Word Search

Catching spam email messages is easy using lexical analysis on the typical words and phrases used by the spammers. The problem of this approach is that it can result in catching large amounts of legitimate business email. Three main issues need to be addressed in creating an effective spam solution are:

1. The performance of the lexical analysis engine. If you are looking for a large number of words and phrases in a long document, processing power and memory will be consumed. The result is a delay in delivering the email.

2. The actual words and phrases used in the detection phrases are crucial. The desire to catch "suspect" text has to be balanced against the possibility of false detection. For example, the typical spam phrase, "earn up to $xxx per" could appear legitimately in a business email such as "unless we earn up to $100 per transaction we cannot make a sensible profit". Just because a defined phrase has been found doesn't mean a spam message has been found.

3. What to do once spam is found. The possible steps are to quarantine the spam, send the spam to a reviewer or send the message onto the intended recipient marked as possible spam.

IP Address Blocking

This is a crude method of blocking spam and is not recommended. To perform it, the IP address of the spam source is entered in a blocklist of IP addresses. By blocking the IP addresses of those email gateways, you will block a whole range of legitimate email.

Email Address Blocking

If you have a nuisance source from a common domain, you can block it without blocking the whole domain.

Spoof and Relay

Spoof is a term denoting construction of an email message that appears to come from someone other than the apparent sender. Spoof is a difficult issue to address, as on the internet there are a whole range of legitimate reasons why IP addresses and domain names match up.

Relay refers to the bouncing of email off other servers to:

• Make the email appear to have originated form a particular domain

• Conceal the source of the sender by bouncing off several servers

• Send email to a large number of recipients at the expense of someone else's bandwidth

The problem associated with relay is that it can make identification of spam mail more difficult. It is especially useful to deal with relay, because it will be beneficial to spam and spoof problems anti-relay fixes the IP addresses and domains that can send email from your relay quoting your domains. This means that spammers can't bouce email off your relay purporting to be you unless they belong to your domain.

Extracted from 'Spam, spoof and relay' by Andy Harris, from Content Technologies. http://www.mimesweeper.com.au

Taking Action – Reporting and Blocking Spam

Reporting Spam

There is so much spam that it is impossible to eliminate it all. However, there are some things you can do to stop specific spammers. Sending directly to the spammer is usually unwise, since even if they provide a real email address, you are only letting them know that your own address is valid, so they can turn around and sell it to other spammers. You need to send it to the provider it came from. Since spammers often falsify their headers, this can be difficult to determine, but there are ways to do it. The easy way to report spam is with SpamCop at http://spamcop.net/.

DIY Spam Blocking

If you would like to track and report spam yourself, first you need to view the FULL headers, which include much more information than just the usual From, To and Subject lines. How you do this depends upon the software you are using.

Pegasus: Choose "READER" from the options menu bar. Listed as an option is: "Show all Headers".

Netscape: Choose "OPTIONS" from the options menu bar. Listed as an option is: "Show Headers", then choose full headers.

Eudora: Open the message. Under the title bar are four options. The second from the left is a box which says "Blah, Blah, Blah." Click on that and all headers will be shown.

Outlook Express: Open the message. Choose "File" from the options menu bar. Listed as an option is: "properties". Another window will open, showing two tabs. You want to choose the one titled "Details". Then cut and paste the headers into the message you want to forward.

Pine: "H" displays full headers and "F" will forward the message which you are currently displaying. (NOTE: you must have headers enabled to view them. From the main menu, type "s" then "c", scroll down to "enable-full-header-cmd" and mark it with an [X], then hit "E" to exit and save.)

Once you figure this out, you need to look for the lines that say something like:

```
Received: from somefakedomain.com (cust34.dfw.tx.domain.com
[206.99.115.1])mail.netwiz.net (8.8.5/8.8.4) with SMTP id OAA00238
for <you@netwiz.net>; Sat, 4 Jul 1998 14:06:36 -0700
```

There may be several entries like this, where the mail is relayed through one or more other servers, in which case the last one is usually the one to look at, although it is also a good idea to inform those providers that they need to disable relaying.

Some spammers will also stick in false headers to fool you. The address in parentheses is where it really came from. Sometimes this name is also falsified, but the numerical IP (Internet Protocol) address in the brackets [] is always correct. You can find the true name (if any) from the IP address by using NSLookup.

TIP

Looking at their web page is a good way to find out if a domain belongs to the spammer or to an innocent provider

If this does not work, or if the spammer has their own domain, you can find the provider by using TraceRoute, which you can do from a DOS prompt in Windows 95/98 using the tracert command. Versions for other OS's are available on the web and you can also traceroute from Yahoo!

You can usually look up who owns the IP address, including their email address, if they're in the US, by consulting the American Registry for Internet Numbers (ARIN). Just enter the host name or IP.

Then you can take the last part of the name shown and send the letter, including the detailed headers. Almost all mail servers have a postmaster mailbox. Most large providers also have an abuse address, so you might try sending there. For instance, if the hostname is cust34.dfw.tx.domain.com, try sending your complaint to postmaster@domain.com or abuse@domain.com. Sometimes the spammers have their own domain, so you will need to figure out the provider looking up their domain name from InterNIC, if it ends with .COM, .NET, .ORG or .EDU.

Looking at their web page is a good way to find out if a domain belongs to the spammer or to an innocent provider. If there is a web page URL listed in the spam, you want to be sure to let their web-host provider know, as well, by sending a copy to them using the same tools listed above.

If the URL lists an IP address, e.g. http://208.136.106.5/etc., you can find the provider using the methods shown above.

If the URL lists some long number, e.g. http://3498600965/etc., you can find the IP address in Windows by typing "ping" and the number in a DOS window.

C:\WINDOWS>ping 3498600965

Pinging 208.136.106.5 with 32 bytes of data:

Blocking Spam

Most mail programs today, including Netscape, Outlook Express and Eudora, allow you to use filtering rules to automatically delete spam after you download it. Check the documentation for your software to find out how to do this. An article on how to filter using Eudora is on the following page.

NetWizards can also block spam before you download it by bouncing all mail that does not contain your username. This is not perfect, as some spam may still slip through and you may not get some legitimate mail such as from listservs, or if you have a forwarding address or alias, but it can stop 99% of spam and a bounced message will be sent to the sender explaining why it was rejected.

This article was provided by NetWizards http://www.netwiz.net

To request spam blocking services, send email to stopspam@netwiz.net

How to Regain Work Productivity and Filter Spam Using Eudora

Bulk unsolicited email can significantly lower productivity and the amount of work that gets done each day. To regain control of your email it is relatively easy to filter emails not addressed to you personally into a special mailbox using Eudora Pro.

By setting up a folder called "Hold for Review" to automatically transfer emails that are not personally addressed to you, you can filter out almost all spam.

Of course, not all emails that are not personally addressed are spam, such as most email newsletters and email discussion lists. That's why we filter to a "Hold for Review" filter as opposed to simply trashing them. However, it only takes a moment to go through and determine which ones are the exception and which ones are junk.

Step 1: Download Eudora Pro. If you don't already have copy it can be obtained from http://www.eudora.com

Step 2: Creating a spam mailbox

1. In Eudora, click on "Mailbox", then "New".

2. Name the new mailbox "Hold for Review" and do NOT tick the "Make it a Folder" box.

Step 3: Programming a Filter

1. Click on "Tools" then "Filters".

2. Place a Checkmark in the "Incoming" box, and then click "NEW" in the lower left corner.

3. Now click on the button to open a dropdown menu by where it says: "Header".

4. Select "<< Any Recipient >>"

5. Scroll down in the box underneath and click on: "doesn't contain".

6. Next to where it says "doesn't contain" put your email address, such as yourname@abc.com

7. Now move down the screen to where it says: "Action". You can program up to five actions that Eudora will perform if it detects an incoming message that meets the criteria you have just programmed into the filter. Let's program it to automatically transfer these messages into our Hold for Review mailbox.

8. Click on Action, then select "Transfer To". Click on the Grey bar and then select the Hold for Review mailbox you just created.

9. We recommend putting and keeping this filter at the very end of your filter list. That way, if you use "Skip Rest" on any or all of the filters above this one, the message will not get to the spam filter. Otherwise, a message can be filtered from "In" to "I-Sales" (for example ;), and then from "I-Sales" to "Hold for Review".

10. The last thing you'll need to do is save this filter. At the top of the screen, click on "File" and then "Save".

Now your Incoming email will be filtered for any messages that don't contain your personal email address in the To field of the message, and those messages will automatically be transferred to your Hold for Review mailbox without you even seeing them.

TIP

Here's a way to prevent the spam robots from automatically collecting your email address from an HTML page and maybe even from email publications and newsgroups. When you enter a mailto in a webpage, format it as follows: mailto:%20yourname@yourdomain.com

It works just fine when someone clicks on it, but when the robots pick it up they end up with an invalid address

---

This article was reprinted with permission from US-based Multimedia Marketing Group, an online marketing agency with offices in London, Oregon and New York. Further info and an email list on anti-spam techniques can be found at http://www.mmgco.com/nospam/ or by emailing info@mmgco.com

Turbo Charge Your Business With Email

By Troy Rollo

M ake a mistake in your email marketing campaign and you could lose 32% of your customers forever. That's the figure revealed by a study into consumer attitudes to email marketing by Cognitiative, Inc, an internet marketing consultancy firm in downtown San Francisco. This figure refers to the reaction of customers who receive sales-oriented email from a vendor they have dealt with before.

"One-third of all respondents say they dislike [unrequested] sales-oriented email so much that it actually makes them avoid the vendor who sends them. Companies may actually be losing business by taking this type of marketing action," Cognitiative says.

There are easy ways to avoid this — in fact if you do it right you can have 85% of your customers subscribing to your email and find that they will complain when they don't receive it. Around 17% of your customers have a reversal of attitude if they get to make the decision themselves.

Don't Breach the Rules

Bigger problems can occur if you send unrequested sales material to people you have never dealt with before. This is a breach of the Acceptable Uses Policy (AUP) of most Internet Service Providers. The AUP forms part of the contract with the ISP and a breach can result in your internet services being disconnected without notice.

It will also do significant damage to your image, with recipients putting your business in the same category as pyramid schemes, illegal products and pornography.

If you send email to large numbers of people who haven't asked for it, that email constitutes "Unsolicited Bulk Email" (UBE, aka "spam"), and the person or company who does it is called a "spammer". You can use email for effective marketing without spamming if you follow some simple rules.

Firstly, never send any email to large numbers of people you haven't had any dealings with before. This includes lists you build yourself and lists that other people sell you. There are a lot of con artists on the market who will try to sell you a list and tell you: "This is a list of people who have said they would like to receive email about products like yours." Don't believe these claims. An email address list like that is far too valuable to sell — the people who really have such lists sell services to get access to the list and never ever sell the list itself.

How to Find Customers

If you want to get access to new customers via email, use one of the opt-in services to do this. These services actually build lists of people who have sought the services out and asked to receive advertising email on specific subjects. These services are pure gold and can get you phenomenal response rates and no risk of being accused of spamming. The grandfather of all such lists is PostMaster Direct, which started in 1996 and now has over 3,000 active lists on different topics. You can find more opt-in services by searching the web for "opt-in email advertising services".

If you want to send announcements to customers, you need to make sure you are getting to all customers who want to receive your messages and none who don't.

This means asking if they want announcements when they supply their email address. While some sites use a check-box to do this, people can miss a check-box, so you can never be sure if they actually made a choice. A better way is to use radio buttons with no default - that way if the customer doesn't make a choice, your form can detect this and ask them to make the choice again. You should have three options on your web form:

1. "Send me announcements"

2. "Send me only critical announcements"

3. "Send me no announcements, ever".

The difference between "announcements" and "critical announcements" is that critical announcements are the non-marketing announcements you need to make because of something unexpected. For example, if your business is sold, you might feel obliged to let customers know that their details are about to be transferred to another business. This is a "critical announcement".

Use a Private List Manager

While this is fairly straightforward to do yourself, you might want to use the new "WhiteHat.com" service. WhiteHat.com can manage your private list for you, making sure that it is run in such a way that you can be assured you will get the maximum possible number of customers signing up, without risking upsetting a single one. The board of WhiteHat.com includes majority control by non-executive directors who are prominent consumer advocates against spam, so you can be confident your lists will be run using the most current best practices for such lists.

For more information on how to avoid damaging your business through making mistakes in email marketing, visit http://www.caube.org.au/ – the Coalition Against Unsolicited Bulk Email has information and links designed specifically for businesses who want to use email for marketing.

References

Whitehat: http:www.whitehat.com

Post Master Direct: http:www.postmasterdirect.com

Cognitiative Inc: http:www.cognitiative.com

Troy Rollo is from the anti-spam lobby group Coalition Against Unsolicited Bulk Email which can be found at http://www.caube.org.au

Direct Marketing – The Consumer Code

By Rob Edwards

The Australian Consumer and Competition Commission's (ACCC) authorisation of a Code of Practice for direct marketing, including world best practice for consumer protection in e-commerce, discourages spam in three ways:

1. By requiring any Australian Direct Marketing Association (ADMA) member making offers by email to provide a simple means for recipients to decline any further offers;

2. By requiring the organisation to remove a consumer's contact details from their marketing list on request (spammers don't respect such requests);

3. By requiring the same levels of consumer protection that apply to other methods of commerce. This includes being totally open about what sort of personal information the company holds, for what purposes it is used and how it collects, uses and discloses that information.

ADMA was the first industry body to take on world best practice in Australia, as determined by the Organisation for Economic Cooperation and Development (OECD) and to make compliance mandatory.

We have backed this up with an independent complaints body that will monitor compliance. Those who argue a higher standard than world best practice simply jeopardise the competitiveness of Australian business.

It is a mistake to think we can put a stop to the spam problem simply by barring

Australian businesses from using email to attract new customers. The reality is that the "spammers" out there will ignore any such regulation. And Australian business will be put at a competitive disadvantage in the global marketplace.

The solution to the spam problem lies in better monitoring by ISPs of content flowing through their systems.

Industry leader America Online has successfully pursued high-profile legal action against spammers and has also made considerable progress in using technology to filter out unwanted messages. Other ISPs ought to follow the example.

It is also worth keeping in mind that more than 70% of spam reaching Australian consumers originates in the US. All the more reason to work through international bodies like the OECD to try to solve the problem.

The Australian Direct Marketing Association have issued Online Marketing Guidelines covering spam and email marketing which are included in the opt-in permission marketing chapter.

Among ADMA's recommendations are that email marketers should identify emails clearly as solicitations and disclose the marketer's identity, provide consumers with the opportunity to opt-out via email and help educate consumers about ways to protect their privacy online.

Rob Edwards is from the Australian Direct Marketing Association
http://www.adma.com.au

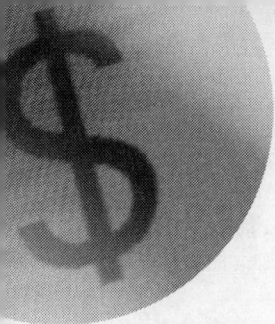

It's Curious That Spam Rhymes With Scam

By Tim Phillipps

I t should come as no coincidence that the word "spam" rhymes with "scam". If you're an email user, you may have discovered that suddenly you have become very popular. Unfortunately, your electronic in-box is not full of greetings from long-lost friends. Instead, it's piled high with commercial messages from complete strangers. Many are asking for money and promising very attractive returns if you part with your hard-earned cash for just a short while.

Welcome to the world of high-tech "chain letters", where an unwanted message can reach thousands of people anywhere in the world, just by the click of a button.

Although some of these messages are from legitimate marketers and investment companies, many are simply from scam artists who make promises they have no intention of keeping.

The Illegalities

The US Federal Trade Commission's warning about high-tech chain letters is sound advice. "These schemes are almost always illegal and the majority of people who participate in them lose their money. Delete the message."

It pays to remember that if an investment on the internet seems too good to be true, then it probably is. Giving your money to someone on the internet just because they ask for it is exactly the same as giving it to someone in the street.

If you don't know who you are dealing with and there is nothing to back them up, then you could be taking a great risk.

ASIC believes the same problems can occur on the internet as in traditional business. You can avoid being ripped off if you make the same checks and take the same precautions as you would for any other investment.

Checklist for Rip-Offs ✔

ALERT

Giving your money to someone on the internet just because they ask for it is exactly the same as giving it to someone in the street who does the same

- Always obtain independent advice from a licensed adviser when considering any investment;

- Only invest in schemes that have a registered prospectus and;

- Check with the ASIC to see if the person promoting the scheme is licensed;

Potential investors can visit the ASIC website at www.asic.gov.au to carry out a range of checks;

- The "Internet Safety Checks" give tips on what to check before investing in internet-based schemes;

- The "Company Search" will let you find out if the company you want to invest in actually exists and if its is an Australian entity. The search will also give you a list of documents lodged with ASIC, including whether the company has a prospectus;

- You can check if your adviser or authorised representative is banned from giving investment advice or if a company director is disqualified from managing a company. They will be on our banned/disqualified register;

- You can also check to see if your broker is licensed and if your responsible entity (formerly known as a trustee) has a securities dealers license.

At the time of writing this article, Tim Phillipps was the director of electronic enforcement for the Australian Securities and Investments Commission, the federal consumer protection regulatory authority. http://www.asic.gov.au

Also on the ASIC website are the Gull Awards, which offer a monthly $50 cash prize given to consumers reporting outrageous, far-fetched or unbelievable financial scams. The scams are updated regularly and tell many a cautionary tale. If you think you have a scam worthy of a Gull Award, email ASIC a brief summary to gullawards@asic.gov.au

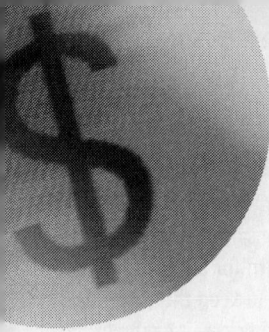

Internet Share Scams – A Case Study

The Australian Securities and Investments Commission (ASIC) in August 1999 joined with the US Securities and Exchange Commission (SEC) in a campaign to stop internet-based free share offers. At the time, ASIC had been receiving complaints about "free stock offers" received by email from an American entity called "FreeBanCo".

"FreeBanCo" or the Free Banner Exchange, described itself as a marketing and advertising group that hosts banner advertisements for a variety of goods and services.

Free Stock Offer

This "free stock offer" was designed to attract a large customer list and more visitors to the site. Most people complaining recognised the email as worthless unsolicited junk mail and chose to ignore the emails. However, many of the complainants were upset that the so-called "free-stock offer", designed like a pyramid-style chain-letter, was referred to them by their friends and workmates hoping to get a larger slice of the action themselves. The offer required people to give personal details to FreeBanCo, which would then be used for any purpose, including being sold to "spam" marketing promoters.

Yahoo Held up as Example

The emails tempted recipients by reminding them of the great wealth earned by the lucky investors who got in on the ground floor of Yahoo! Consumers were encouraged to register their details with "FreeBanCo" in return for a credit of five shares in the entity, should it incorporate and float publicly. To keep the chain mail nature of the exercise moving, FreeBanCo also offered a further credit of three shares for every person referred.

The "free stock offer":

• promised free shares in a yet-to-be formed company;

• enticed customers with promises of potential future wealth;

• used references to net-based success stories like Yahoo! and Microsoft;

• invited the customer to register on the promoters website; and

• promised customers greater share credits for referring others to the site.

The Moral of the Story

"In the cyberworld there is significant value in your own personal email address. Unless you are prepared for a bad case of spam (unsolicited email) in the future, then do not give it away - especially when you receive nothing in return," said Tim Phillipps, ASIC's director of electronic enforcement at the time. "A promise of share credits in a company that has not yet been incorporated and may never list publicly is a share in virtual unreality!"

ASIC told the SEC that the offering may have been a breach of ASIC law as it invited or offered securities in a proposed corporation, hawked securities of a proposed corporation and took part in referral selling, which is illegal in Australia.

This article was provided by the Australian Securities and Investments Commission, the federal consumer protection regulatory authority. http://www.asic.gov.au

Email Scam Prevention Sites

Australian Securities and Investment Commission (http://www.asic.gov.au)

South Australian Office of Consumer and Business Affairs
(http://www.ocba.sa.gov.au/scamex.htm)

NZ Ministry of Consumer Affairs
(http://www.consumer-ministry.govt.nz/news.html)

Federal Trade Commission (US)
http://www.ftc.gov/bcp/conline/edcams/mailbox/index.html

Industry Canada recalls and frauds
(http://strategis.ie.gc.ca/SSG/ca00553e.html)

Internet Fraud Watch (http://www.fraud.org/internet/intinfo.htm)

NZ Securities Commission (http://www.sec-com.govt.nz/)

Scam Busters (http://www.scambusters.com/)

US Postal Service (http://www.usps.gov/fyi/welcome.htm)

The Better Business Bureau (US and Canada)
(http://www.bbb.org/alerts/index.html)

Phone Busters (http://www.phonebusters.com/)

Trade Practices Act
http://www.austlii.edu.au/au/legis/cth/consol_act/tpa1974149/

Managing Your Email

Introduction

So, You've Got Email?

Email is a business communication power-tool with almost unlimited and wonderful potential. However, it can also be potentially lethal for business (as will be explored in subsequent legal and security chapters), not to mention a cause of unnecessary and unhelpful workplace stress and frustration.

The key to getting the most out of email is adopting and applying good email management practices.

Elaine Lawrence's article "Using Email for Office Efficiency", illustrates how email must be handled with respect. She strongly advises organisations to ensure that workplace electronic communication policies be put in place and enforced and that workers be trained in the efficient use of email.

Policy Pointers

Business email etiquette should be tailored to suit your particular needs. The nature and size of your business, email traffic volume, flow and types of use plus personnel profiles, technology requirements and legal responsibilities should all be taken into account when formulating policy.

In "How to Draft a Good Email Policy", Peter Leonard sets out the legal principles and parameters that should be included in an electronic communications policy.

In "Staying out of Court – Leave a Clean E-Trail", Chris Morris urges companies to apply basic technical and management safeguards to keep their e-documents out of trouble. As a model of an email management guide, the National Australian Archive's "How to Manage Email Records" details why email needs appropriate management and offers email rules for business transactions and security. "Successful Email Policy Implementation" outlines steps and do's and don'ts for a low impact modification of your business' email culture.

The critical importance of email is that it is your customer's voice and, in Jim Sterne's "How to Answer Email", he stresses the importance of giving email the attention it deserves.

Managing Mailing Lists

Many of the problems associated with the management of email involve the use and misuse of email lists. Obviously an understanding of different types of email lists can assist not only in selecting and running lists, but also in the establishment of good email list management practices.

If You're Having Trouble: You're Not the Only One!

Despite the benefits of email, some businesses either don't like it or don't use it properly. This can be because of poor "netiquette", inconsiderate response times, inappropriate uses of the email system, disorganised checking practices and so on.

To give an overview of the factors involved in email business use, this chapter includes research and surveys on common business patterns and attitudes towards email.

Frequently asked questions addressed include the following ... What is email used for and how often? Is it a time sapper? What do people love about it? What do people hate? What works? How soon is a reply required? How soon should a reply be sent? What stresses people out?

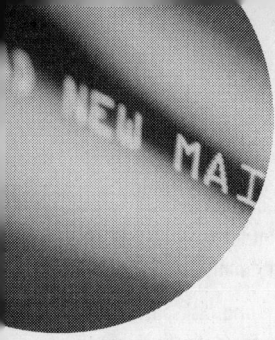

Successful Email Policy Implementation

By By David Jones

What follows are the suggested steps to introduce email policy enforcement. To ensure that business email is a priority, organisations must also act on less desirable email activity, so that it is managed, reported on and captured where necessary. The methodology of these steps is designed to be of "low cultural impact" to your organisation and incremental to slowly modify the email culture.

Step 1. - Commitment

The most important step is to ensure that upper management in the organisation is aware and understand the technical risks and the legal risks to the organisation (and the directors) of email abuse. They must also be committed to the successful deployment of this technology and understand the organisation's position on personal usage of email. Involve HR or operations management because policy is primarily a people issue (rather than technical).

Step 2a - Policy

Introduce your email usage policy, ensure distribution to all email users. Ensure the staff managers at each office are aware and supportive of the initiative and the business reasons driving it.

Step 2b - Educate

It is important to not push the "big brother" aspect, just the acceptable business usage aspect. It is important to state that email scanning is an automated process and nobody has the time or inclination to review all internet emails.

It is worthwhile giving people examples of wasted bandwidth and diskspace and tell them that often important email can't get through because other non-business related email takes the majority of the internet connection.

BOLD: Step 3 - Monitor

Monitoring is critically important. "Policy without monitoring is like laws without police" is the catch-phrase. You will always find more surprises than expected; on average EmU Tech's EmU software finds around 35-40% of email is graphical and around 70-80% is non-business related.

BOLD: Step 4 – Start Blocking

Implement low impact rules:

- File Size Restriction

- Isolate (block) WAV, AVI, MPG files - these are virtually never business oriented.

- Add a corporate disclaimer to outbound email

- Stop and Check EXE's - examine how many people are using self-extracting EXE's in the course of their work.

- Regularly monitor the accuracy of the rule triggering, refine your rules so that you are not getting too many false "hits".

Step 5 – Reminding Employees of Policy

Implement an extension of Step 4. When an isolated email occurs, automatically send replies to the sender suggesting they contact the recipients that the email will be delayed if the email is legitimate (or not delivered at all if it has suspect content). ALWAYS make the email reply courteous and never assume the monitoring is perfect, the reply should suggest that you contact the Email Security Administrator if the email rule triggering is incorrect or invalid.

You may wish to add an inbound footer - stating the email has been scanned. This is an effective method of reminding employees and educating new employees of the important of the email usage policy. The footer should direct the reader to the location of the policy on the organisations intranet.

Step 6 – Review and Refocus

The suggested delay between each step is probably about two weeks, ensuring you receive a progress report on the cultural impact from the staff managers at each office. You should be aware that Step 5 in particular may have a negative reaction among staff and implementation of automatic deletion should be undertaken with care.

Examine the data and experience, report on users who are trying to get around the system, allow HR to take control of the daily monitoring and review of messages. Allow your IT staff to refocus on IT issues.

Do...

✔ Implement a corporate "Acceptable Internet Usage Policy".

✔ Implement a policy deployment program that regularly reminds employee's of the policy's existence.

✔ Deploy internet monitoring and filtering systems to automatically block offensive and illegal internet content and reinforce acceptable internet usage policy.

✔ Inform employees that web and email are corporate assets.

✔ Inform employees that web and email are automatically monitored.

✔ Educate employees that internet policy and monitoring is for the protection of individual staff and contractors as well as the employer from legal liability.

✔ Automatically append every email with a legal corporate disclaimer.

Don't

✗ Send, forward, download, display, print or otherwise disseminate material that is sexually explicit, profane, obscene, harassing, fraudulent, racially offensive, defamatory or unlawful.

✗ Assume that other people will share the same sense of humour that you have and send joke emails at work. Apply the "reasonable persons test".

✗ Write hasty and emotive phrases in emails and if unsure as to the suitability of the message, request a second opinion from a colleague.

✗ Send emails which may contain computer viruses such as games or other executables.

✗ Assume that corporate email is private property. Email and web usage can be audited at any time.

David Jones is Technical Director of EmU Tech Pty Ltd, an Australian based company specialising in email policy software and consulting. EmU Tech is a silver sponsor of this handbook. http://www.emutech.com.au

Using Email for Office Efficiency

By Elaine Lawrence

B illions of emails are sent around the world each day and it has become a key driver behind the explosion of electronic commerce. It is used to transfer company data orders, invoices, word-processed documents, spreadsheets and CAD files between business partners saving time and the expense of sending paper communications.

Email represents a vital opportunity for business. Because email is rooted in a network, email addresses can be archived easily, can be mailed to in bulk and the domain part of the address can be analysed to detect patterns of usage. However, these same opportunities can also cause business problems unless this extremely powerful tool is handled with care.

Email Monitoring by Companies

A survey conducted by PricewaterhouseCoopers in 1998 found that 13% of Australia's top 100 companies regularly monitor email and that about 6% read messages. About 15% of companies that monitor do not tell their employees. In the United States about 27% of companies monitor workers' email. Although there is no legal prohibition to such email monitoring, organisations need to be aware of employee privacy protection and employee relations issues.

Using Email for Customer Support

Many organisations set up an email facility on their website but do not provide the staff to support these email facilities at a high level. In fact, some companies which are using call centre staff to answer emails are finding that costs can balloon if email and multimedia chat sessions are handled manually. The Rockwell company has automatic internet communications studio and email management solution. This product:

- links a company's web site to a call centre for real-time chat or video interaction with customers;

- manages the way email is answered.

Customers expect and deserve quick responses to email queries, yet many online companies fail to reply to emails at all. The replies need to address the questions posed. Companies must match the email expectation by implementing a staffing model that matches the customers' needs.

It is also vital to treat every email as a sales opportunity, but this should be used cautiously - customers do not want to get a flood of email. If you want customers to visit your website, include your Universal Resource Locator or web address in your email.

For handling global email, the business might consider email translation packages that allow for the creation, sending and receipt of emails in over 90 languages, for example Tango Mail from Alis Technology at http://www.alis.com.

TIP

Set aside a specific time to read and respond to email

Tips for Handling Email

As employees are finding email so pervasive, it is a good idea to train them in effective email coping techniques.

- Set aside a specific time to read and respond to email. Scan it for anything that has to be handled immediately and then deal with other emails at a set time. Use email to filter tasks. There are some tools to help with this, such as the Interactive Mail Access Protocol (IMAP). This allows for better control over the way messages are delivered. Instead of having all the new email messages delivered from the email server onto the user's computer at once, IMAP gives the user greater flexibility in interacting with the inbox. The user may choose to only download the subjects of the new email messages, then select and download only relevant messages. It also allows the user to see what files are attached to an email and then decide which ones to download. Obviously this is ideal for users receiving email over slow connections, for example a laptop computer accessed via a mobile phone.

- Do not use automatic notification of email, as this will encourage the user to be constantly dipping into the email. Lucent Technologies have developed a web-based message management tool which offers a mobile, unified application for voice, fax and email services via the internet. Users can view all types of messages in the mailbox. Other useful features are:

- voice message playback, creation, reply and forwarding via phone or multimedia computer;

- fax message viewing, printing and forwarding with voice messages;

- messages addressed by mailbox number, user name or distribution list;

- administrative functions such as creating greetings, editing distribution lists and changing passwords. through a phone or computer;

- viewing, creating, forwarding and replying to email;

- Use folders to sort and store email – the user should have a filing system that makes sense of the business imperatives of the job. Do not store things that you have to do in your inbox – make up a to-do folder or a pending folder and clear the inbox. A continually filling inbox can stress a worker;

- Avoid conflict situations with email. It is important that staff are trained in "netiquette" and realise that many people dash off an angry reply via email without thinking through the business consequences.

Elaine Lawrence is a lecturer at the School of Computing Sciences at the University of Technology, Sydney. http://linus.socs.uts.edu.au/

How to Draft a Good Email Policy

By Peter Leonard

An electronic communications policy which forbids certain employee conduct and says that illegal acts by employees won't be tolerated is vital to minimise the new risks posed by e-commerce.

A good policy should take account of the difficulty of asserting central control and direction over the use of electronic communications and therefore sets parameters within which employees should act.

In order to reduce liability risks from employees' use of the internet for unauthorised or illegal transactions, the policy should expressly categorise certain conduct as "prohibited" and as outside the scope of their employment contract.

It should also state that the organisation "cannot be said to approve an employee's illegal act" and should further include:

- an introduction explaining why it is necessary to read the policy and the sanctions imposed for breaches;
- a statement allowing the organisation to monitor email to comply with law;
- a prohibition on specific content for transmission or download;
- an outline of which material cannot be transmitted externally;

- an explanation that corporate identifiers must be used and a warning about invasive data collection by some website operators;

- requirements and cross-references to advertising and marketing guidelines;

- a warning on possible application of trade practices and fair trading laws;

- restrictions on, or requirements for the use of, encryption or secure transmission channels for particular types of transactions;

- if intranets or extranets are used, the conditions for employees access;

- guidelines for storing and using passwords and other security data (which should be regularly rotated) and examples of good and bad passwords;

- a warning that deleted files can be recovered for use in litigation;

- requirements for regular back-up and other record-keeping; and

- restrictions and procedures on financial transactions, eg transfers of funds.

Peter Leonard is a partner at law firm Gilbert & Tobin, Sydney.
http://www.gtlaw.com.au

Staying Out of Court – Leave a Clean E-Trail

By Chris Morris

As the 1999 Microsoft monopoly court trial showed in the US, even the powerful Bill Gates himself appeared nervous when discussing embarrassing email internal messages during evidence. And witnessing the experience made other executives nervous about email too. As of course it should.

Such high-profile cases reinforce that whatever you transmit by email or any other e-document can be used against your company in court. And while it might seem that e-trails pose the same legal liability issues as paper trails, the risks and exposures are actually greater. Companies must apply basic technical and management safeguards to keep their e-documents out of trouble, even if they can't keep them out of court.

Technology provides the virtual certainty that not just email but also business presentations, strategic plans or any other e-documents can be used against a company in court. And, as litigiousness grows, the likelihood that this will happen is high.

The Microsoft trial last year focused the attention of organisations on the email its employees send.

E Now Stands for Evidence

In many ways, the legal liability companies incur in their use of email is barely different from the liability they bear for any document produced in the course of doing business. But email, or any other electronic document, poses its own problems and responsibilities – of which many companies are unaware.

Three features make email different from other mediums for business communication:

First, it's easier to scan 20,000 email messages than 20,000 pieces of paper to look for specific words and phrases.

Second, people tend to express themselves freely (often too freely) in email.

Third, getting rid of all electronic evidence of such unguarded moments is extremely difficult.

Most companies generally write their own document-retention policies, largely to avoid spending the money and using up space. However, such policies typically don't include email, because disk storage is easy and cheap. In addition, individuals like to keep archives of their work. Unfortunately, if the company is sued, five or 10 years' worth of stored email could be subject to unwanted legal scrutiny. And at this point, deletion is not even an option.

Smart companies now include e-documents in their formal document-retention policies and delete old electronic records as fast as they can. But there's no guarantee that you can ever delete 100% of the emails you want to remove. Every email ends up on a PC, on a server and on the internet gateway. There are also countless other technical explanations why a digital ghost could come back to haunt you. And, of course, there's the paper trail once it's printed.

Protection from liability is not a simple matter of knowing how to get rid of email. It requires diligent technical management that covers all communications formats throughout their life cycle. It also requires close attention to employee behaviour. Below are some of the basics:

- Write a policy for email. The policy should state clearly what constitutes proper and improper use of email and the consequences of sending inappropriate messages. It should also acknowledge that the company knows there will be some personal use of email.

- Educate employees. It's amazing what people write in an email without thinking. Companies must emphasise the risks in creating and sending email. They must make clear to all users that email is a business tool and that each person has a responsibility to use it in an efficient, effective, ethical manner.

- Watch your language. Policies should define what the organisation considers to be within the bounds of acceptable communication. It's also good to provide

TIP

Your email policy should state clearly what constitutes proper and improper use of email

additional coaching on the use of appropriate language. The GartnerGroup's rule of thumb is never write anything in an email you wouldn't say in a business meeting. Rules should apply to internal and external documents. Even a seemingly innocent executive habit of using military metaphors to discuss business strategy can hurt, as Microsoft found out the hard way.

- Monitor employees' email. This is guaranteed to raise the spectre of Big Brother and the suppression of free speech. Legally, it's a moot point. It must be done if policy and legal protections are to have teeth; but the issue is how to do it. At the outset, employees must know their email is subject to monitoring, which must be carried out intelligently – random efforts are ineffective and inefficient. The best method is an automated system that checks all your company's email, examining patterns to identify potentially damaging content and looking for general email abuse.

- Delete regularly. Regular electronic housekeeping consists of routine procedures which remove most email messages after a period of time. This period should be long enough not to compromise current business needs but short enough to assist in managing space on the disk. Users should be able to keep certain messages out of the clean-up process by filing them into a long-term retention area. Without this, users will simply copy messages to their desktop.

Chris Morris is a vice president for research in the GartnerGroup's Sydney office. http://www.gartner.com

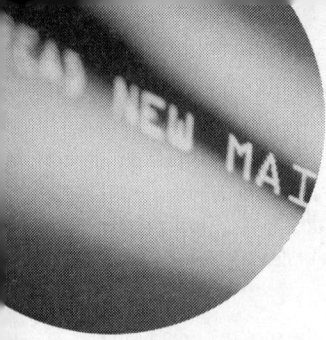

How to Manage Email Records

By National Archives of Australia

Email has an image problem. In many organisations it has been introduced as an informal or even personal form of communication, with no regard to alerting staff of the implications of its use in the business environment for creating records.

Electronic mail users need to educated to understand that electronic messaging systems are provided at work to support official business. Messages created in the course of duty are no more the user's property than is a business memorandum or a letter.

The personal use of messaging facilities (creating personal records) is a matter for agencies to determine. Both business and personal use should be articulated in agency policy, guidelines and training.

Email is recognised as a legitimate source of evidence and can be the subject of subpoenas, discovery orders and applications under the Freedom of Information Act 1983, in the same way as any other records.

Advantages of Email

- quick, informal and easy communication;
- cheap (much cheaper than using the telephone for any call or the post for a letter);

- more immediate dissemination of reports and other documents;

- logs the time of an exchange of messages (although not always the correct time);

- one person can send the same message to a number of people simultaneously (one to many method of communication); and

- not as intrusive as the telephone.

Disadvantages of Email

- the same message can exist in multiple locations, leading to storage problems;

- informality can lead to sloppiness;

- allows publishing via the internet without approval from supervisors;

- easy to edit/alter;

- lack of systematic management other than deletion for space requirements;

- deletion does not mean destruction (deleted messages can be retrieved); and

- multiple copies of messages or attached documents can be easily printed and filed, which is expensive in both time and paper.

Email Rules

Organisations need to operate within a basic set of email rules. The following rules are an example which may be used in agency guidelines.

Business Transactions

1. Email systems are provided primarily for business communications and important transactions should be printed out and filed on the relevant file or captured into an electronic recordkeeping system.

2. Keep copies only for ongoing business reasons and delete material only in accordance with agency guidelines.

3. Do not use the paper filing system as a dumping ground for electronic communications; only file on paper the important documents you have initiated or received.

4. Avoid printing out documents sent for information.

5. Avoid making hard copies of reference material such as articles or long documents that have been published elsewhere and can be cited.

6. Email systems are the preferred method of inter-office communication.

7. All email is the property of the organisation.

8. Avoid putting into email messages what would not be put into office memos. Use sarcasm and humour with care; they can be very easily misunderstood without the benefit of accompanying body language.

Security

1. Email systems must not be used to transmit any classified, staff-in-confidence or commercial-in-confidence material, except where these systems have been established for such a purpose and have appropriate controls.

2. Ensure that passwords are used on all email systems.

3. Scanned signatures should not be used in any circumstances (they can be cut and pasted to give the appearance that a document was signed officially).

4. Email communication is not private. Administrators and other authorised personnel have access to the system and occasionally so do unauthorised personnel. You can use email for private messages, bearing in mind the rules for email management and exercising caution. Any opinions you express via external email, where they are not related to the conduct of business, should be noted as your opinions and not those of the organisation.

5. Ensure that email systems, like all other electronic systems, are backed up and maintained in accordance with systems management standards.

The National Archives of Australia's Guidelines on Managing Electronic Messages as Records can be viewed in full at:
http://www.naa.gov.au/govserv/techpub/messrecs/EMGuide

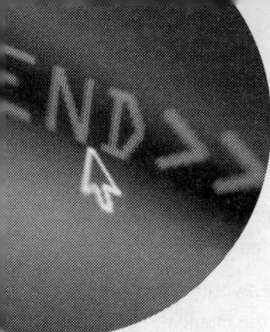

How to Answer Email

By Jim Sterne

E mail is the glue that cements the internet together. Unless you're surfing from a friend's computer or at a public access terminal, you have an email account. As wonderful as file transfers are and as great as the web is, it is email that is the common denominator and the most powerful tool we have.

Email is Your Customer's Voice

The rest of your website is looking from the inside out, trying to give them what they need. But electronic mail is from the outside, coming in. It's your connection to the outside world.

Give Email the Attention it Deserves

People know that email will sit patiently and wait for the recipient to read it. But the sender isn't as patient as the mail sent: There is an expectation that an email will secure a reply within 24 hours.

If it's critical, a customer will usually call. If it's a contractual issue, they'll send a fax with its inherent status as a legal document. But if it's merely important; a product question, a service modification or a clarification of some kind, they'll send an email. They don't need an immediate answer, but they're not doing it for their health either. They expect an answer and the ball is in your court to get it for them.

Frame Answers Carefully

One thing is clear: the more information your customers can get, the easier they can get it and the faster they can get it, the happier they will be doing business with you.

While an individual email may be boneheaded, may seem like a waste of time, or may be filled with invective that rubs you the wrong way at the moment, the issue is very important to that individual.

Customer E-Service

Most companies with a large customer service situation have implemented some sort of call management system. There are countless help-desk and call-center software packages on the market today. A quick trip to Yahoo! will turn up a long list. To make the most of them, make sure there is a link between incoming email and your current back-end systems.

Even if it's as simple as cutting and pasting messages from your email system into a problems reporting or customer tracking system, you're better off than relying on individuals to manage the system by hand. Conversely, there are serious gains to be realised by automating the hand-off. In fact, there's every reason in the world to automate the whole process from start to finish. The email turns into a service request. The service request is routed by problem type or geography or support service level. The solutions are sent to the customer and stored in the corporate knowledge base for future reference.

Carry Out Random Checks

Just as you'd monitor the occasional call to the call centre, read the occasional email to make sure it lives up to your standards of courtesy, clarity and charity. Send out email to those who have been helped by your team and ask them outright if they are satisfied with the help they received. After all, when your customers want to talk to you, they deserve that you listen as closely as you can. And keep wearing those customer-coloured glasses.

Jim Sterne is an author, speaker and consultant with Target Marketing, a US marketing & customer service strategy consulting company.
http://www.targeting.com

Managing Mailing Lists

Using Email and Mailing Lists

The advantages of email can be remarkable. Email lists and mailing list managers can cut the unit cost of a $2-per-piece direct mailing to $0.001 or less, replace the company newsletter with a low-cost alternative, eliminate the interoffice memo and even reduce group teleconferences.

With the pervasiveness of the internet, local area networks and email, mailing list managers can help disseminate information far more quickly and inexpensively than any other comparable technique.

Just like sending private email from one person to another, a list server can send the same message to hundreds or hundreds of thousands of people immediately.

This method of targeted mass communications makes sense for your customers, your website visitors, your prospects, your investors and your office colleagues.

Better still, email's combination of speed and ease of use actively encourages people to talk with each other.

Mailing lists don't merely enable interaction, they encourage it!

What Mailing List Managers Do

At the most basic level, mailing list manager software controls the distribution of messages to list members.

A message to the list is processed by the server and forwarded to all list members. The list manager is responsible for the day-to-day workings of a mailing list. It controls who is on the list, when and how messages are sent and the availability of the list to the public.

Smart mailing list software adds to this by including other mechanisms. Bookkeeping jobs such as bounce management are critical. List managers can be overwhelmed by email that is continuously returned because of a bad address or a slowdown somewhere on the Internet.

Good list software can also be instructed to refuse to accept a subscription request from someone until they send an acknowledgment confirming that they do indeed want to be on the list.

The list server can perform other functions as well. It can act as an archive for information, keeping copies of all messages sent to a specific list. This archive can be used either strictly as a "paper trail" (for instance, on a product development list, to keep an accurate timetable of when ideas were recommended), or as a reference library which can be accessed later.

More advanced list managers also include reporting tools for analysing message activity, from how many people on the list actually got the message, to how many responses a given message received.

Discussion vs. Announcements

There are two basic kinds of lists: announcement and discussion lists.

Announcement Lists

An announcement list is sent from a single source to multiple recipients, with responses directed back to the sender.

This type of list has a one-to-many and many-to-one structure and is used for:

- email marketing;
- customer communications;
- e-commerce;
- online newsletters;
- new product releases;

- e-zines;
- fan communications and;
- many other marketing, information and notification tasks.

An announcement list will normally have one or more people designated as list managers, who are allowed to post announcements to the list. Responses from subscribers to the list may be sent to the list manager or directed to another email address.

Discussion Lists

In contrast, a discussion list is one on which messages to and from members are seen by all. Each person can respond to each other, send messages to the list and engage in conversations. These lists have a many-to-many structure and are used in office work groups, personal interest or hobby groups, professional association groups and similar groups. Once the list is established, all members have the ability to post to the list.

Discussion lists typically have far more traffic than comparably-sized announcement lists and a robust list manager will be a requirement.

Moderated vs. Unmoderated Lists

Discussion lists, where everyone is encouraged to talk to one another, come in two basic varieties: moderated and unmoderated.

Moderated Lists

A moderated list is one in which all messages must be approved by the list maintainer (also known as the list owner). Messages go first to the list owner and then on approval are forwarded to the list membership.

When every message has to be individually approved, the list manager needs lots of free time or list traffic volume will sink to the floor. For some people, moderated announcement lists work well. With someone always in control of what's seen and unseen, a moderated mailing list is best used for low-volume, sharply focused mailing lists.

Unmoderated Lists

With an unmoderated list, all messages go directly to the membership, without being checked for relevancy.

For open conversations, unmoderated lists make sense. They also are the most popular kind of discussion list. This is due, in part, because moderated lists take much more time to administer.

Closed vs. Public Lists

Announcement and discussion lists can be either closed or public.

Closed Lists

A closed list has a restricted membership. For example, a manufacturer would restrict a list to customers who own a certain product, or an association would make its online newsletter available to members only.

Public Lists

A public list is available to anyone who chooses to subscribe. Lists that offer product information from a website, fan lists for football teams or musicians and newsletters that address the needs of an interest groups would all be public lists. Public lists can also have restricted memberships. Here, the list owner has to approve any prospective list member.

Using Email Lists – Direct Marketing

Announcement lists make a good direct marketing tool. Direct email marketing has the same goals and uses the same methods as postal mail direct marketing.

The key differences are:

• Speed – email marketing is much faster

• Cost – email marketing is much cheaper

• Perception – how the audience expects to be treated

How the Audience Expects to be Treated

Postal bulk mail in the form of catalogs, credit card offers or supermarket sales arrives at most homes daily and has a place (even if grudgingly granted) in the lives of recipients. Its cost for delivery is also borne by the sender.

Email direct mail, because its delivery costs are paid by the recipient and his or her internet service provider, and because it takes time to download, review and delete, must depend on the willingness of the recipient to receive it.

If someone comes to your site and signs up for news on your consulting service, he or she will expect and welcome the news when you send it.

Sending the same announcement indiscriminately to everyone whose email address you can find will not be welcome. It will be spam – the indiscriminate, unsolicited bulk delivery of email.

Effective email marketing also depends on being able to target your message, personalise the email and measure the results. While you could use a standard list server for direct marketing purposes, they don't keep or give you enough information about your list members and its results.

TIP

List management systems offer a great way of getting not just your message but also your brand in front of people on a regular basis

Using Email Lists –Customer Communications

Mailing lists are great for keeping in touch with customers. Rather than spending thousands of dollars on printing and postage when you announce a new product or a special offer, simply send email. No fuss, no extra costs. Your customers will appreciate it. With email, there's almost no delay between sending the message and its receipt and you can deliver links to special websites in the body of the email message.

Customer support is also easier with email lists. If a customer discovers a problem that may cause trouble for others, you can simply send out a single message to everyone on the mailing list, rather than wait for each customer to contact you in turn with the same problem.

Using Email Lists –Marketing

List management systems offer a great way of getting not just your message but also your brand in front of people on a regular basis. For example, a newsletter filled with information that your customers can use gets your name in front of potential customers again and again.

The key is to have a message that people will want to see. A simple ad won't do it, but, if you give the right people real content, they'll read it and slowly but surely they'll start remembering your brand in conjunction with good advice.

Using Email Lists –Online Sales

Amazon.com, the highly-successful online book dealer, automatically lets its customers know via a list server when their order has been shipped. They also notify customers of similar books that may be of interest, making it easy and convenient for them to make additional purchases. Not only are the customers pleased, but this personal service touch gives them more reason to think positively about the product and make them more inclined to do business with Amazon again.

You Can Do the Same for Your Online Sales

Of course, an ordinary email-address-only list manager isn't suited for this job. A database-enabled email server that is linked to a customer database is required. Then, all customers who have purchased a certain product, or all those expressing an interest in a product, can be notified and updated when the product becomes available.

Using Email Lists – Internal Communications

A major stumbling block in any office process is a breakdown in the flow of communication. The misplaced memo, the forgotten meeting, even being accidentally forgotten in an email loop – all of these can cause delays in your work schedule. With mailing lists, this can be avoided. Every message is immediately transmitted to every member of your work group or office who is on the list. There are no paper copies to be lost, and no one is left out of the loop.

Moreover, mailing lists facilitate group discussion. Rather than calling a meeting every time someone needs feedback on an idea, group members can post their thoughts and reactions to the list. Everyone can respond with their comments at leisure. An ongoing discussion can take place even while other work is being done (rather than only during long meetings).

Unlike other forms of communication, lists are not time dependent. People contribute their ideas when they're at their best, and not when a meeting coordinator demands their attention.

Excerpted from: The Guide to Managing Your Email Communications, reprinted with permission from MessageMedia. http://www.messagemedia.com

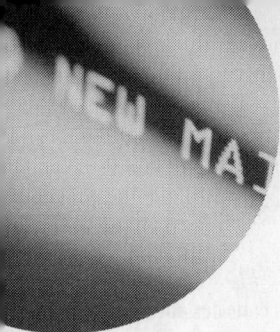

How to Avoid
Time-Wasting Email

A survey of email business users from 200 Australian companies in November 1999 that a great percentage of emails are counter productive and, in many cases, cause irritation, office tension, breakdowns in inter-office relationships and negative comments.

There is a gross misuse of email, with personnel using email for purposes other than work such as for sending jokes, internet games, video and picture files. No wonder email is considered by many to be a waste of time.

Broadcasting email to entire companies is happening with monotonous regularity and there have been several reports of personnel accidentally broadcasting private and confidential information to parties who should not receive that information. Inevitably, this has caused embarrassment to the parties concerned, resulting in the initiator of the email being fired and legal action being started.

Some of the problems with emails include emails being written in capitals, not answering emails, lost emails, not responding to email, using email as a replacement for verbal communications, delays in responding to email because of company policy and unnecessary footers at the base of emails.

Out of their research, Sterling Software prepared the following business email etiquette tips and the lists of responses to common email loves and hates.

Email Tips

- Do not use "blanket" broadcasts unless it's relevant to all recipients.

- Compress files before attaching them to emails.

- If you have a large attachment (and it's an internal email), consider putting it in a central location on the LAN and indicate the path and filename in your email.

- When scheduling a meeting, use an Appointment/Meeting Request, not a standard email message.

- Don't flag a message as "urgent" unless it really is!

- When sending jokes, etc, preface subject lines with "Humour:" and mark the message "low priority"

- Use "Voting Buttons" where appropriate.

Email Loves

- Customer email indicating progress.

- Wit, charm, use of written (rather than spoken) language.

- Jokes.

- Email with websites embedded.

- Inventive signatures.

- Praise for individuals.

- Short emails.

- Useful information about website updates (short and concise).

- Knowledge-sharing emails.

- Brief and direct emails – tell me quickly what you want and get the hell out of here.

- Microsoft Outlook and meeting scheduling, what a dream! You can see where everyone is and book almost everything. So quick and easy.

- The speed at which I type now, because I spend all day writing emails.

- I like emoticons!

- I like typos!! (from Brian the Brain).

- I like emails encouraging and praising me! (-:

- Pertinent notes (corporate news, or local); staff-related information; wins/losses stories.

- Very time-effective way of distributing information to a large number of people.

- Email makes it easier to send information globally.

Email Hates

- Emails written in capital letters.

- Important emails .... which are not addressed to me!

- Emails with large attachments ... unzipped!

- Unanswered emails!

- Nonsense and more flow-on nonsense that keeps circulating (gross mis-use of email).

- People hitting the "reply all" function before engaging their brain!

- Emails with tasks embedded in them.

- Undeliverable mail.

- Address hassles.

- Zip file attachments.

- "Reply to all" on general mailings where comments do not need to be distributed.

- Emails with attachments which can be viewed on the web or network server.

- Long emails.

- Irrelevant emails.

- Too many emails. We don"t talk enough to each other and revert to lengthy, "bouncy" conversations, rather than arranging a meeting to talk to each other. Can often be as time-costly.

- Increasing expectation that a reply will be received quickly. Life doesn't revolve around email. It's checked in the morning, once during the day and towards the end. If it's that urgent, call me!!!

- Too much of the day spent reading and writing email. Not enough time to do my proper job! I'm going to start closing outlook during the day more often.

- Dumb internet games or long joke emails. I love a good joke, picture or movie file, but if it takes ages to read it or run it, forget it. I'll come back to look at it in 2001.

These tips have been provided by Sterling Software, an Australian information technology company. http://www.sydney.sterling.com

Patterns of Email Use by Australian Executives

InterBiz Solutions' monthly Vox Pop survey of Australian chief financial officers (CFOs) in July 1999 focused on the use of email at home and in the office. All respondents were CFOs within small-to-medium enterprises with annual organisational revenues of between A$20-50 million. Forty CFOs took part in the survey.

• The survey found a high use of email by CFOs with the majority of respondents indicating they believe email is a positive productivity tool.

• The majority CFOs responded that they checked their email five or more times per day and very few people six percent replied that they defer acting on or replying to received emails until later.

The Questions and Results

Question	Yes
1. Do you use email at work?	82%
2. Do you use email at home?	42%
3. If you have email at work, do you check it:	
a) once per day	18%
b) a couple of times per day	18%
c) 5 or more times per day	64%
4. Once you have read an email, do you tend to act on the request or send your response	
a) immediately	48%
b) later	6%
c) depends	46%
5. Do you use email to communicate primarily	
a) within your own organisation	52%
b) to external suppliers, customers and partners	6%
c) both	42%
6. Do you believe that overall, email is a positive productivity tool?	
a) Yes	76%
b) Yes, but overused	24%

This article provided by interBiz Solutions a Computer Associates division designed to assist worldwide clients, suppliers and partners in capitalising on e-commerce business opportunities. http://www.interbiz.cai.com

Business Email – Be Prompt and Don't Snub the Customer

Various business surveys have shown that a prompt email response time is essential to customer satisfaction. A survey by Morgan&Banks in 1999 found that email snubbing, whereby the person or organisation requires several emails from the sender before replying, rated number five on a list of causes of undue stress.

Australian Business Advisers Pty Ltd (ABA) also conducted a survey in April 1999 to measure the responsiveness of Australia's largest 100 companies to an email question – "What is your corporate headquarters' address?"

"The speed at which responses were received provides an insight into the emphasis that is being given to online customer service by corporate Australia," said Rod Brooks, senior consultant at Australian Business Advisers, which conducted the survey.

Nearly 1/3 of Firms Can't be Emailed

While 80% of Australia's top 100 companies (by market capitalisation) have a website, seven companies (nine percent of companies with a website) could not be contacted by email in the survey from their site or made it so difficult that most visitors would be unable to make email contact.

Therefore, a total of 27% of Australia's largest companies could not be contacted by email. This result is similar to a survey in the US of Fortune 100 websites conducted by Brightware, Inc (www.brightware.com), which found that 26% of the 100 largest companies in the US could not be contacted by email from their website.

Quick Responses Generate Loyalty

Yet another survey of online customer service expectations by Cognitiatives, Inc (www.cognitiatives.com) found that customers prefer responses to their email questions within a few hours, but that response times of one day are acceptable.

Their study also found that exceeding customers' expectations can result in extreme brand loyalty.

"To date, online customer service has been so dismal for many customers that when vendors are actually responsive, the customer is surprised, delighted and loyal for life," explained Laurie Windham, founder and chief executive officer of Cognitiative.

Most Companies Reply in a Day

The survey by Australian Business Advisers found that 49 companies (61% of companies with a website) responded within one day.

This compares with a survey in October 1997 of 50 large Australian organisations conducted by APT Strategies, where 46% of organisations responded within 24 hours of an email request.

"Australian companies appear to be improving their email responsiveness, but most companies are still falling short of customer expectations," added Brooks.

Five companies utilised an autoresponder to acknowledge receipt of the query, but only one set a time-line for responding (and kept to that time-line).

Interestingly, whilst 27 Australian companies (34% of companies with a website) responded within three hours, only 15% of US Fortune 100 companies responded within three hours to an identical question in Brightware's survey.

But before Australians begin crowing about being faster than the Americans, it should be noted that not all the survey results were rosy.

Eleven Australian companies (14% of companies with websites) failed to respond within four weeks, compared to 10% of US Fortune 100 companies in Brightware's survey. And many of the companies that did not answer are consumer-oriented.

However, these Australian results were much better than a survey of 325 British websites conducted by Buchanan EMail Limited (www.buchanan.co.uk) where 38% of websites did not respond to a simple email query!

Beware of Demanding Customer Details

In the survey by Australian Business Advisers, 29 Australian companies asked for personal information before they would answer any email question:

- For 22 companies, this information (eg phone number, address etc) was optional but rarely was this revealed.

- For seven companies, the form required personal details before the email could be sent.

- Only four companies with a website had any privacy policy on their site.

"It's a misguided attempt to gain marketing value from customers," says Chuck Williams, CEO of Brightware.

"Imagine walking up to an employee of a retail store with a simple question and having them require you to fill out a form. You would just leave, which is what people on the net do."

"Or false information is given," added Brooks.

Keep Replies up to Standard

Perhaps the most surprising finding of the Australian Business Advisers survey was the lack of professionalism of the replies.

"Only 37% of the email replies contained either a name or title and the company name," said Brooks.

"A number of replies contained an address but no indication as to who sent the email or which company it came from. And some emails in their "From" field had names such as "Francis:" "Corporate Affairs Internet Address", and "Internet Machine". If a company name was not in the email text, then it was not always easy to determine where the email came from. Whilst email is expected to be less formal than snail mail or fax, it would appear that many companies either do not have or are not enforcing a standard signature file as part of their email policy," concluded Brooks.

Conclusion

"Overall, many Australian companies are becoming serious about online customer service, but most firms still have a long way to go to meet customer expectations," said Brooks.

About the Survey

A single surveyor, Rod Brooks, in April 1999 visited the websites of the top 100 Australian companies by market capitalisation (as listed on www.kangaroo.com/companies – please note this site appears to be undergoing redevelopment and may not be available). Eighty of these top 100 companies had websites. To enable a direct comparison with US forms the survey methodology was identical to that of the Brightware survey (www.brightware.com).

At each site the surveyor made reasonable efforts to find the simplest way to send a simple email question, either through a general email address or email form. The surveyor noted who did and did not accept email and also noted whether the website permitted the submission of a simple question without requiring information other than name, email address and the question at hand. The common email query – "Could you please tell me what is your corporate headquarters address?" – was sent during business hours to those sites that did accept email (or web form submissions). The time the question was sent or submitted to each site was recorded, as was the time an answer was received. It is acknowledged that other surveys at different times may yield different results.

Rod Brooks is a senior consultant at Australian Business Advisers.
http://www.abaconsulting.com.au

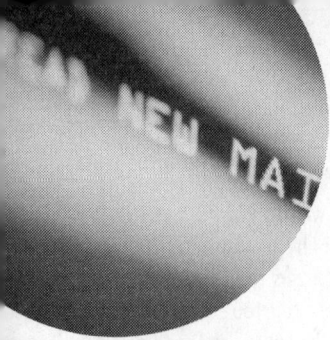

Email – Help or Hindrance?

By Morgan and Banks

Email is Crucial to Business Communications

The increased use and misuse of email has meant that some businesses see email as a challenge to their already time-starved operations. Some may feel overwhelmed with the amount of mail traffic, while others may feel time is wasted checking emails too frequently or waiting for email responses.

A Morgan&Banks Job Index Survey conducted between August and October, 1999, asking bosses if they felt the increased use of email was a time-sapper, found that larger businesses considered email more of a drawback than small and medium sized businesses. See Table 1.

As well as differences of attitude toward time spent dealing with emails between different sized businesses, there are varying degrees of opinion on whether email is a time-sapper between different industries. See Table 2.

TABLE 1, Organisation Size

Do You Think The Increased Use Of Email Is A Time Sapper?

Organisation Size	Yes	No	Did Not Answer
Small (< 20 employees)	38.4%	60.3%	1.3%
Medium (20 – 200 employees)	45.5%	52.2%	2.4%
Large (> 200 employees)	56.7%	42.5%	0.7%
Total	47.2%	51.3%	1.6%

TABLE 2, Organisation Type

Industry	Yes	No	Did Not Answer
Advertising And Marketing	40%	60%	0%
Chemical And Oil	50%	50%	0%
Construction And Property	30%	70%	0%
Electronics	50%	50%	0%
Engineering	36.4%	63.6%	0%
Financial Services And Insurance	61.2%	34.7%	4.1%
Food And Fast Moving Consumer Goods	36.8%	63.2%	0%
Government	57.1%	35.7%	7.1%
Health And Medical And Pharmaceuticals	50%	40%	10%
Information Technology	45%	54.5%	0.5%
Legal	83.3%	16.7%	0%
Manufacturing	37.5%	58.3%	4.2
Media	33.3%	66.7%	0%
Resources	50%	50%	0%
Retail	64.3%	35.7%	0%
Services	46.2%	53.8%	0%
Telecommunications	40.9%	59.1%	0%
Tourism	100%	0%	0%
Transport	54.5%	45.5%	0%
Utilities	42.9%	57.1%	0%
Other	33.3%	33.3%	33.3%
Not Defined	56.3%	43.8%	0%
All Industries	47.2%	51.3%	1.6%

SOURCE: Morgan&Banks Job Index Survey August – October 1999.

One conclusion that can be drawn from these findings is that different types of businesses need to tailor their email management practices and policies to suit their business type, size and level of email traffic.

Morgan and Banks is a global human resources company.
http://www.morganbank.com.au

How One Angry Email Triggered an Industrial Dispute

By Jeannie Rea

This is a case study of an industrial dispute at the Victorian University of Technology in 1998, over the suspension of three staff access to email through the university network. The case was eventually successfully resolved through the use of industrial action.

The Angry Email

This dispute was triggered by the academic staff representative on the University Council, Professor Allan Patience, posting a global email that so angered the Vice Chancellor that he wrote to the staff member that his message was allegedly defamatory and suspended the academic's email access.

The Vice Chancellor, Professor Jarlath Ronayne, argued that the use of email *"to harass, intimidate, denigrate or defame any members of the university community, whether staff, student, or member of a university body, such as council, will not be tolerated".*

Some context is required to understand why management reacted so swiftly, strongly – and, in my view, inappropriately:

Professor Allan Patience, the academic who had his email access suspended, sent around a report after each university council meeting.

After the meeting in March 1998, he sent his email report, venting his anger at the council's decision to support the annual leasing of a corporate box at Colonial Stadium for $100,000, whilst at the same time contracting out the university mail service, despite widespread vigorous protest from the university community.

There had been an industrial dispute over the contracting out issue, as well as opposition from the Academic Board on the basis of the loss of confidentiality.

Union Response

The National Tertiary Education Union (NTEU) immediately questioned the removal of Allan's email access, arguing that it was a disciplinary action without any proper process being followed.

Two other staff members were also cut off:

• One had responded to Allan's email with a congratulatory comment, but accidentally sent it globally.

• The other person cut off had sent an unrelated message that probably should have been dealt with in another way.

It is our analysis that these other two staff members were cut off to try and diffuse attention from the content of Allan's email. All those cut off were union members and the union sought to have all the cases recognised as inappropriate disciplinary action. Under the award covering academics, management is obliged to detail the allegations, provide the member of staff with the opportunity to respond and establish a misconduct investigation committee.

University Response

In response to internal university complaints, the university claimed that the three staff had contravened the university's email protocols. However, to the wider community, they claimed that Allan's remarks were defamatory and opened the university to litigation.

What remains particularly absurd about this whole case is that if the university had just ignored Allan's email, it would have remained an internal university debate and the university's unwise financial decisions would not have entered the public arena. Because of their over reaction, not only did the university's disciplinary action hit the mass media both in Australia and internationally, but so did the content of the email. VUT, which is always seeking a higher media profile, now is unfortunately associated with this somewhat bizarre case.

How Was the Dispute Resolved?

The NTEU responded to the outrage in the university and sought to negotiate a resolution with management by threatening a stop work meeting.

The university was prepared to reconnect the staff if they basically admitted that they had misbehaved.

Whilst denying that they had disciplined staff without due process, management did want to resolve the problem without further escalation.

The stopwork meeting, attended by over 200 members, resolved that unless the members were reconnected without conditions, a 24-hour stoppage would result.

Eventually, the members were reconnected, only signing a note acknowledging that they had read the existing university email protocols. A union/management working group was re-established to rework the protocols.

The Question of Intellectual Freedom

Policing email use by management is apparently common practice across public and private organisations.

However, in universities, any such monitoring is immediately questioned within that particular privilege of universities – the concept of academic (or intellectual) freedom.

The issue was taken up in other universities and the media and even raised in state parliament. Top academics wrote letters and articles and commented upon the "attack on intellectual freedom" reflecting increasing silencing of dissent in an increasingly corporate university environment.

There are many employers who do not allow free access to "global" email, particularly in larger organisations. I am also aware that many unions also do not have access. I can only say that this it is well worth campaigning for such access.

Example of Guidelines

The Manufacturing, Science and Finance Union (MSF) is the fifth-largest union in Britain, representing over 400,000 skilled and professional people. MSF is addressing many areas of these areas concern relating to the electronic communications in the workplace.

This is a copy of the access to email section from their Model Digital Facilities Agreement:

Access to Electronic Mail

a) MSF representatives have the right to use the corporate email system for works council/trade union purposes, to send and receive emails both internally and externally.

This shall include the right to send email communications to all employees, subject to this right being exercised reasonably.

There shall be a further right to operate electronic bulletin board or discussion list services within the corporate email service, provided such facilities are technically possible.

b) Employees have the right to use the corporate email system to communicate with their MSF representatives and officials.

c) Employees are permitted to use the email service for non-business use during business hours to send and receive individual emails both internally and externally provided that this is not detrimental to their job responsibilities.

d) The employer undertakes that email will not be routinely read or monitored. Email will be monitored and retrieved only if the employer is legally obliged to do so or has reasonable reason to believe that an employee has committed a criminal offence or serious disciplinary offence or is in breach of this agreement. In these situations, email will be monitored and retrieved only in the presence of MSF representatives.

e) The right of employees to send and receive emails is subject to the following conditions:

i) Email sent must be lawful and not include defamatory or libellous statements.

ii) Email shall not be used as a means of sexually harassing other members of staff. Email shall not be used for sending offensive comments based on an individual's gender, age, sexuality, race, disability or appearance.

iii) If required by the employer, personal email sent both internally and externally shall include a disclaimer to the effect that the views expressed are those of the author's alone and not necessarily those of the company.

Extracted from: "Rights Of Workers To Electronic Access In Workplaces: A Case Study". The full document can be viewed at: www.labourstart.org/itpa/juneconf.shtml

Jeannie Rea is a lecturer in Communication, Language and Cultural Studies at the Victoria University of Technology and the president of the local branch of the National Tertiary Education Union (NTEU). http://www.edunions.labor.net.au/nteu/

Handing Over Email to the Law - Where You Stand

The law can obtain copies of all company emails without a warrant, according to leading telecoms lawyer Allan Collier. He warns that copies of electronic records kept by internet service providers (ISPs) can be accessed by police, courts or other law enforcement officers without them having to obtain a warrant.

If law enforcement officers from agencies such as the Australian Taxation Office, the Offices of State Revenue, the Police Services and State Departments of Primary Industries are investigating a company and wish to search the premises, they must obtain a warrant.

Similarly, they must obtain a warrant if they wish to monitor a telephone line.

But if they want to access emails or other information which has been recorded electronically by service providers in the process of transmission, they can do so without a warrant, Collier, a consultant with Clayton Utz, Brisbane says.

The Telecommunications (Interception) Act 1997 allows disclosure of information that is reasonably necessary for the enforcement of the law. In addition, information recorded by service providers in the process of transmission between parties is not covered by the Act, which only relates to interception while communication is taking place.

"The Interception Act dates back to 1979 and relates to telephones only. It pre-dates faxes and emails and it didn't contemplate what is going on now," Collier says.

"However, a carrier or carriage service provider cannot give copies unless it is ... for the purpose of enforcement of a law imposing a pecuniary penalty, or the protection of the public revenue." This has major implications for e-commerce in respect to trade sensitivities and privacy issues, Collier says.

It also raises issues for employers and employees, as copies of emails, internet access logs and other transactions are also kept by an organisation's gateway computer.

"The Act only applies to carrier or carriage service providers; it doesn't stop employers having access to it. Employees should know that every message has been recorded and that they have given permission," Collier says, adding employment contracts usually include such clauses.

"It can be an effective management tool to track staff activities, but it raises privacy issues, as many people are surrendering their privacy without understanding they are doing so."

SOURCE: E-Commerce Today, Issue 15, October 8, 1998.
http://www.ecommercetoday.com.au

How Emails Can be Requested Under Freedom of Information

A NSW District Court Ruling in October 1998 ruled that emails could be classified as documents under NSW Freedom of Information (FOI) laws. The court decision required the Environmental Protection Authority (EPA) to release internal staff email into the public arena.

The court ruled that 110 emails and around another 100 documents should be released under an FOI request from a residents" group fighting a Port Kembla copper smelter.

The EPA had released 304 documents previously, but judged 236 as exempt under government FOI guidelines. It argued that to disclose some documents would inhibit frankness and candour.

EPA director-general Neil Shepherd had said that traditionally FOI only related to written material. "However, much of the preliminary debate is now carried out by electronic messages and it is unclear how FOI relates to this new form of communication," he said before the ruling, noting that the outcome of the case would further guide the EPA and other agencies on implementing FOI provisions.

In early 1999, the EPA introduced guidelines to set down the appropriate and professional use of email responsibilities, internally and externally.

Don't Ignore the (e)Law

Introduction

How to Keep the Law on Your Side

By Peter Knight and Jim Fitzsimons

The purpose of this article is to identify ways in which an employer may be held liable for the conduct of employees and ostensible agents acting outside the scope of their authority – simply because the employer has provided an email and internet communications network.

Exposure to Liability

Messages that are transmitted externally or internally across the network may cause the organisation to incur liability in the same way as a letter or other correspondence may do. Changes to Australian law, beginning with the Federal Electronic Transactions Act 1999, ensure that email communications will be treated in most cases in exactly the same way as any other written communication.

The difference, however, is that people are far more candid and less thoughtful about email, because it is viewed as an informal means of communication. It is therefore useful to consider some of the potential forms of liability thrown open by email.

Breach of Confidence

A great deal of information is disclosed to an organisation which it must treat as confidential. The recipient of confidential information has a positive duty to the person from whom it received the confidential material not only to maintain the confidentiality of that information, in the sense of not disclosing it to others, but also of not using the information for any purpose other than that for which it was disclosed.

An email user at the organisation might deliberately or unintentionally disclose that information to another person, inside or outside the organisation, not necessarily making clear its origin. This is even more likely to occur, given the propensity of email users to set up mail lists/discussion groups, which may include representatives of external organisations.

Thus, liability may arise in two ways:

– Firstly, by the mere fact of disclosure to a third party in breach of the duty of confidentiality.

– Secondly, by reason of use of the information by another person within the organisation who was not made aware of the restriction on its use.

It is all too easy to send either intentionally or accidentally, for example, the company's marketing strategy to the competition. Disgruntled employees or those leaving for greener pastures may well feel such action necessary and by the time the event has taken place, it is too late for the organisation to take action. Or, for example, most of us have at some stage inadvertently sent an email to the wrong person. Sometimes these mistakes can be irrecoverable.

Defamation

Email and interactive bulletin board services somehow bring out the worst in people. Users and the suppliers of the network vehicle across which defamation may be published must exercise great care to ensure that others are not defamed.

Reputation and personal and pecuniary ramifications for the defamed of losses resulting from a defamatory publication are the essence of the law in this area. Defamation may be defined as a publication that is communicated not just to the plaintiff but to a third person, which is likely to cause the "ordinary reasonable member of the community to think less of the plaintiff, or to shun or avoid the plaintiff".

The ascribing or attributing of a negative quality to a person is called the making of a defamatory "imputation".

Inevitably, our federal system of government has led to defamation being a complex tort, varying in meaning from state to state. In addition, the common law has been modified by statute in most states. However, generally speaking, a written defamation (sometimes called a "libel") is considered much more seriously in many respects.

ALERT

Email and interactive bulletin board services somehow bring out the worst in people. Users and the suppliers of the network vehicle across which defamation may be published must exercise great care to ensure that others are not defamed

The significance for email is that, whereas it is treated by employees as being analogous to spoken communication, like a conversation, in law it is a written communication and is hence considered a most harmful conduct.

Furthermore, some imputations are considered more serious than others. Any suggestion of "unchastity in a woman" will be regarded as extremely harmful. Similarly, imputations disparaging a person's business or professional acumen, or suggesting a person has committed a criminal offence (in emails, people are very careless with notions of fraud, theft and blackmail), or suggesting that a person suffers from a communicable disease, especially a sexually transmitted disease such as HIV will all be regarded as defamatory and harmful. It is precisely imputations such as these which are commonly bandied about in careless emails.

It should never be assumed that malice is a necessary component, nor that truth is a defence.

In addition, anyone who is a party to the publication may be liable, however innocent he or she may have been of the defamatory imputation made. This includes the author, editor, printer, publisher and even the disseminator or distributor of the publication.

A person who provides a network may have a liability for the publication across it of a defamation unless he or she proves that he or she was unaware of the material, was not negligent in not being aware, and had no grounds for supposing that the publication of defamatory material was likely to occur.

Accordingly, an employer must educate the users of the network not to use it to publish hurtful imputations about co-workers or others and actively monitor the network to ensure that defamatory material is not being published.

Copyright

In cases of breach of copyright by those accessing a network, whether by uploading copyright material for re-copying by others or by unlawfully copying such material available on the network, a person who provides a network may be found liable for such breaches of the copyright if he or she "authorised" the infringement.

Simply enabling access to a bulletin board facility will not result in the service provider being found to have "authorised" an infringement of copyright which follows, unless the access or board provider does more to encourage such misconduct.

However, the following warnings must be given:

• It may not be sufficient to avoid liability merely by being passive – inaction may be sufficient where it may be seen as encouraging the misuse of copyright material;

- It will not be relevant that the service provider is unaware of the actual infringement taking place.

- It may not be of any assistance to the service provider that it gains no direct or financial benefit from the illegal copying

- It may not be enough for the service provider to simply include a prohibition in its network access contract or a warning notice on the bulletin board, if that is merely a ritual.

The Federal Government has attempted to address some of these issues in the Copyright Amendment (Digital Agenda) Bill 1999.

Harassment, Discrimination and Criminal Behaviour

Sexual discrimination and harassment laws can all apply to email. Employers owe a positive duty of care to their employees to provide a safe working environment, free from unlawful harassment and discrimination, as well as being vicariously or directly liable for the actions of their employees.

Sexual harassment may constitute not only unwanted affections from a co-worker, but also office pranks such as the sending of offensive material, such as pornography.

And persistent and unwanted humour singling out an individual on the basis of religious, racial or sexual grounds, when it has been previously rebuffed, may give rise to liability on the part of the employer for failing to protect the employee.

Furthermore, in the case of pornographic or offensive subject matter, the use of telecoms facilities such as email to disseminate this material may also constitute a criminal offence for which the supplier of the network may be found liable if he or she was aware that the network was being used in this way.

Contract Issues

Your organisation might also create contractual liabilities, commit a breach of contract, or be negligent by means of an email message.

A contract is not at all dependent upon a single form; a contract can be wholly oral or hundreds of pages long, detailing all conceivable contingencies. Contracts can also be in a mixture of forms, perhaps constituted by a series of letters, together with some oral terms or a series of documents linked together by a "master agreement". Certainly, contracts may be formed by email.

In the absence of any agreement that the arrangement is not binding, if the following elements are present, there will be a binding contract:

1. An offer, which is accepted;

2. Consideration for the promises given (although this is not required in some countries, such as Japan and Taiwan); and

3. Consensus as to the subject of the contract.

So communications made over email, ostensibly as part of some negotiation or other discussion, may lead to binding commitments unless it is made clear that they are not intended to do so. It is quite common for courts to conclude that these represent or are evidence of a binding contract.

Such conduct extends to breaking contracts as well as making them.

Every day, we face questions of binding commitments made by people by email communications, where those people did not appreciate the effect of their email and/or did not have authority to make such a commitment. Remember, the test is not what the employee thought he or she was doing, but what a reasonable person in the position of the recipient of the email would have thought of the email.

Negligence and Misleading Conduct

It should be understood that the potential for "professional negligence" now extends beyond mere lawyers, accountants and other professional advisers.

Any organisation which has expertise or special knowledge in an area may be found negligent where it carelessly provides advice or information within that area of expertise or special knowledge in circumstances where the recipient relies on that advice or information. "Professional negligence" has been found against salesmen, local government bodies, stockbrokers and others, notwithstanding that they do not fall within the traditional categories of professional advisers.

Similarly, even where an organisation does not have such a duty of care, it may be found liable for "misleading or deceptive" information under section. 52 or s.53 of the Trade Practices Act 1974, and equivalent state and territory legislation.

The Myth of Privacy

Users of the organisation's email system within the organisation itself do not have a right to privacy. Junk messages may abuse the system and other messages may harm the organisation's legal rights at a later date.

All information passing through the system may legally be viewed by and disclosed to management, untrammeled by any (legal) concerns regarding privacy. However, common sense and industrial peace, dictate that this should be drawn to users' attention. It is accordingly recommended that a notice to all users appear on a boot-up screen such as:

"NOTICE – all messages transmitted through the email system may be archived and reviewed at any time by [name of organisation]. Sensitive and confidential information should not be sent by email."

Deletion and Disclaimers

The current law of evidence in all Australian jurisdictions recognises electronic records as being evidence which must be produced in court proceedings. As well, such records may be required, as mentioned above, in criminal inquiries or in response to the rights of access to documents afforded the Australian Taxation Office, the Australian Consumer and Competition Commission and the Australian Securities and Investments Commission. But material which is not required to be kept is best destroyed.

Further defensive assistance may be provided by an automatic disclaimer produced by a signature file on every message. The disclaimer would state that the message is not necessarily authorised by the organisation and should not be relied upon without confirmation. However, it should be noted that a disclaimer which is automatic and appears on all messages, even those where it is inappropriate, may soon lose significance and value, although it would not actually be harmful to the organisation's position.

This article is an extract from the paper "Legal & Commercial issues for email & Internet Communications" prepared for Content Technologies by Peter Knight and Jim Fitzsimons who are solicitors at Clayton Utz. http://www.claytonutz.com.au

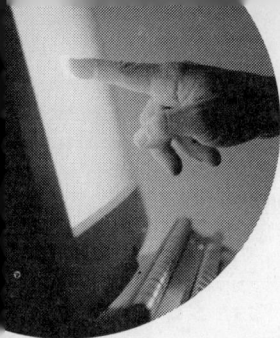

E-Documents in the Courtroom

By Brendan Scott

M uch of the legislation that requires records to be kept was drafted in the dark ages and relates specifically to hard copy documents. For example, "documents" must be kept and they must be kept in "writing". If you want to produce the document, you must do so by producing the "original" or a "photocopy". Do these terms mean anything for an electronic document?

What are originals? How must they be kept? Unfortunately, there are no easy answers. Separate requirements are created by separate acts and each act requires a separate answer. Whether your storage methods are legal can only be determined on a case-by-case basis. As a rule of thumb, Commonwealth legislation is very good at permitting the retention of documents in an electronic form and state legislation leaves something to be desired. However, that said, there are some circumstances in which the Income Tax Assessment Act does not permit documents to be retained electronically.

How Long Do Records Need to be Kept?

Even where legislation does permit documents to be held electronically, there may be serious obstacles to their retention in practice. Retention periods are characteristically extremely long in the scale of technology evolution. Three or five years is not unusual. But back in the real world, few of us have any experience with electronic documents more than one or two years' old. This is especially the case where those documents have been stored on a specific medium. Will 31/2" disks be obsolete in five years' time? What about your documents stored on those disks? You'll probably be in breach of the legislation.

Encryption Problems

Similar issues arise where documents have been encrypted or compressed. If the encryption, archival or compression program is not available to recover the document, then you're in breach. Therefore, great care must be taken when disposing of old archival utilities! Even where the retrieval procedure is merely very difficult to implement, there will be a serious question as to breaches. For example, records encrypted for security purposes which cannot be readily decrypted may be considered by the Tax Commissioner to be not "reducible to writing in English" in breach of the Act.

State Rules

In order for a document to be admitted into evidence in a court of state, you must comply with the requirements of the Evidence Act of that state. For example, litigation conducted in the Supreme Court of New South Wales will need to comply with the New South Wales Evidence Act. By and large, the Evidence Acts around Australia take a similar approach to most issues, but not on the admissibility of electronic documents. Many have problems with admitting them into evidence.

At a minimum, a company storing records electronically will need to look at the Evidence Act of their own state to assess their own level of comfort. Some states are particularly good – NSW, the ACT and courts of a federal jurisdiction. Others such as South Australia aren't.

The South Australian legislation, while once progressive, imposes significant barriers to the admissibility of electronic evidence. It forces you to keep certain records of the operation of the computer during the whole period. It is not possible to contract out of these requirements or to otherwise negotiate them away with the other party to the litigation. This makes them doubly dangerous. The South Australian Government has successfully lured a number of electronic businesses to locate their data processing centres within South Australia. If your business is one of them, it is imperative that you review the provisions of the South Australian Evidence Act and ensure that you comply with them in respect of all computers in your data centre.

'Original' Documents

The "Best Evidence" rule says the original of a document must be produced and only if this is impossible may a copy of that document be produced as evidence of its contents. In the electronic realm, the copy stored in the hard drive of a computer is the "best evidence". Even print outs are "copies" within the meaning of the best evidence rule. So there is a problem.

In litigation, as in life, it's often a case of Murphy's Law. If an electronic document is damaging, you can expect it will be admitted. Indeed, email is routinely admitted into evidence in proceedings in Australia and there are a number of cases in the United States in which email has come back to haunt people, even long after it had been deleted. This is because email has a resilience unheard of in the world of paper documents. An email itself can be deleted and the email program itself removed from a computer and yet the contents of the email can still be recovered.

Checkpoints

If the lessons to be learnt from this article could be distilled into four points, they would be:

• Check the statutes – are your electronic documents legal?

• Check the Evidence Acts – can your electronic documents be admitted?

• Develop a communications policy (part a) – Loose lips sink ships;

• Develop a communications policy (part b) – email should be properly centralised, backed up and migrated as necessary.

Extracted from 'Soft Words, Hard Targets: Admissibility of Electronic Documents', by Brendan Scott, who is a partner at law firm Gilbert & Tobin, specialising in e-commerce and the law of electronic document management. http://www.gtlaw.com.au

The Legal Risks of Doing Business Online

By Ann Slater

The key problem with doing business on the internet is its intangible nature. There are no physical records, unless they are created separately. Even then, there are no originals. What we have are a collection of electromagnetic fields that comprise communication, data and records.

It is precisely this intangibility that generates hazards. Computers crash. Systems and networks go down. Data gets corrupted or simply disappears. Messages get lost in transit. The result can be that:

- communications do not get made;

- communications get made to the wrong person;

- records get lost or destroyed;

A failure to communicate will be fatal to conducting business in any environment. Internet auction site eBay was subject to significant outages for various hours at a time in 1999. This has been disastrous to eBay's profitability as an online auction forum, as well as for the vendors and potential purchasers of products listed on eBay.

Remedies

The impact of communications not being made from a legal perspective include the absence of offer and/or acceptance in forming a contract; the misunderstanding of the terms of a commercial transaction, due to the lack of communication of some or all of the terms and the inability for negotiations to proceed or the misperception that one party does not wish to proceed with a transaction.

Steps that can be taken include asking for confirmation of all key communications made in the context of a transaction, sending confirmation of all communications received and including a summary of your understanding of the proposed terms at key steps in the transaction.

Hazards associated with a failure to communicate with the right person include potential breaches of privacy or confidentiality principles, if the communication refers to sensitive information of either the sender or the intended recipient and potential action for breach of confidential information, disclosure of trade secrets or similar claims.

Steps that can be taken to minimise the legal risks include seeking confirmation of the receipt of key communications, including confidentiality notices in communications similar to those that usually appear on fax cover sheets, stating that the communication may include confidential and personal information and seeking its return and deletion if it is misdelivered and using security measures such as encryption, digital signatures or SSL (secure internet communications) protocols.

In the case of records getting lost or being destroyed, there is potential liability for failing to comply with taxation laws or accounting standards, the inability to support or defend invoices, claims made against customers or suppliers, or claims made by them and the inability to properly perform obligations under the transaction. Steps that can be taken to minimise this risk include backup, backup, backup, either electronically or in hard copies; and storing data contemporaneously in various locations such as on a computer network, as well as on a hard disk.

Jurisdictional Issues

"Jurisdictional issues" refers to issues which arise when business is conducted over the internet spanning more than one state or country. The identification of which law applies to a transaction is a key issue that is not always easy to determine.

Impacts

Potential impacts of conducting business over the net across different jurisdictions include:

- the transaction may not be recognised or enforceable in the other jurisdiction, due to different laws of contract;

- the transaction may be subject to different or additional taxes, customs or duties; and

- the transaction may be illegal in the other party's jurisdiction.

Steps That Can be Taken

- Clarifying in terms of the transaction that the other party is responsible for any taxes, customs or duties that may apply to the transaction in their jurisdiction;

- seeking confirmation from the other party that they will be legally bound by the transaction in their jurisdiction and that the transaction is not illegal; and

- clarifying that the law which applies to the transaction is the law of your jurisdiction.

Ann Slater is a Partner at PricewaterhouseCoopers Legal, and specialises in Intellectual Property, Technology and Media. She is based in Sydney.
http://www.pwclegal.com.au

Does Copyright Apply to Email?

By Elizabeth Barnett

N o particular steps need to be taken to gain copyright protection for email – the work does not need to be registered, nor does it have to bear the © symbol. If a work meets the basic requirements of the Australian Copyright Act 1968, it is automatically protected. (Only Australian law will be discussed here. However, emails sent internationally may be affected by quite different copyright rules to those which operate in this country.)

Generally, a copyright owner is entitled to take legal action if someone exercises their rights without permission. The requirements most relevant to emails are:

• **The work must be reduced to material form.** That is, it must exist outside its creator's mind in a more or less permanent way.
An email which has been printed out or hand-copied has clearly been reduced to material form. However, the Copyright Act specifically provides that works which exist only in electronic form are also protected.

• **The work must be original.** This does not mean that it must be novel or inventive. It means that the work must originate from its purported author and not merely copy another work.

Someone who simply forwards an email authored by another person, or pastes it into another document, would be unable to assert copyright in that content.

- **The work must be non-trivial.** It must have been produced through some degree of skill or effort. However, protection does not depend on any aesthetic or other inherent merit.

Single words, short phrases and titles are extremely unlikely to be protected by copyright in their own right. Raw information is not protected by copyright, but a way of presenting information which required some effort may be. So emails which are more than a few words long are protected by copyright

Who Owns Copyright?

The basic rule is that copyright in a work is owned by the person who put the work in material form. There are important exceptions:

- Different rules apply to particular types of copyright subject matter, such as cinematograph films, sound recordings and broadcasts.

- If certain types of artistic works are commissioned, the person placing the commission, not the person creating the work, owns the copyright.

- Copyright can be sold or transferred to someone else. The copyright in a work and ownership of the actual work are two different things from a legal point of view. Copyright can only be given permanently to someone else expressly in writing, signed by the person transferring the copyright.

For example, usually an artist will continue to own copyright in a painting even after the painting is sold.

- Employers automatically own copyright in works produced by employees in the normal course of their duties. (Special rules apply to journalism.)

Employees are not entitled to use their employer's copyright for private purposes, nor can they take copyright documents with them for use by a new employer.

- However, an independent contractor owns copyright in anything she produces in the course of performing her contractual obligations. Typically, someone engaged under a contract for services and more or less able to determine how they perform those services is a contractor.

Thus a client will not automatically own the copyright in draft specifications emailed to it by an engineering consultant, even after paying the consultancy fees.

- Employees' and contractors' copyrights can be managed through specific contractual terms. For example, terms of employment might include compliance with corporate policies, which in turn might provide that the company owned copyright in all material generated using its technology. A consulting contract might provide that copyright in all material produced by the consultant in the course of performing the services vested in the client.

How Long Does Copyright Last?

Copyright is very durable. In most cases, a published work will continue to be protected by copyright for 50 years after the death of its author. Works not yet published at the time their author dies can be protected almost indefinitely. Emails are therefore protected for 50 years after the death of their author.

ALERT

The penalties for breach of copyright range from court orders to paying damages

---

What Infringes Copyright?

Copyright is breached by exercising any of the copyright owner's rights without permission (preferably explicit). Material posted on the internet, for example, is not necessarily freely available for use or exploitation. It may have been posted without permission. In any case, the copyright owner may be happy for others to view the work but expect a fee for using it in certain ways – or may not want it copied at all.

The most common form of infringement is copying. "Copying" does not mean making an exact copy of the entire work. It may still breach copyright to copy only part of a work or if the copy has been altered to make it appear to be different to its source. Even a small portion of a work can be significant, such as the signature bars of a tune or the best-known lines of a poem. Basically, in using others' material as inspiration, you should create something entirely new in order to avoid infringing copyright.

If you include in emails substantial or important content of a work created by another person, and you do not have unambiguous permission from them to do exactly what you have done, you may have breached their copyright. The penalties for breach of copyright range from court orders to take (or stop) certain action to paying damages or an account of profits gained through the illegality. In particular circumstances, criminal sanctions may also apply.

Liability for Others' Infringement

Generally, employers are legally liable for wrongs committed by their employees in the course of performing their duties. Thus an employer may be held liable for an employee's breach of copyright in emails sent in the course of business, whether or not the employer directed the employee to do the infringing act or was even aware of it. In some circumstances, one may be liable for authorising a third party (such as a contractor or business associate) to infringe someone else's copyright.

Downloading from the Internet

You copy a work if you save material from the internet onto a hard drive or storage media, print it, or send it in an email. Doing so without permission breaches copyright. (Copyright is not infringed simply by visiting a website.)

Implied Licences

In some circumstances, you do not need to have express permission to use someone else's copyright work. Usually, this applies if the work has been created on your behalf for a particular purpose – you are entitled to use the work for that purpose. The extent of the permitted purpose may not always be clear.

For example, you would be entitled to use graphics emailed to you by an artist for a particular advertising campaign in preparing and running that campaign, including copying the images into advertisements and forwarding the email internally. You might not be entitled to have the graphics registered as a trade mark for general commercial use unless this had been expressly agreed with the artist.

ISPs' Liability

Internet Service Providers have been vulnerable to arguments that each time one of their users breaches copyright in Internet material, and each time the ISP caches or mirrors a website, the ISP has also infringed copyright. Recent changes to Australian law now make it clear that an ISP is generally not liable if it simply provides the infrastructure or technology which was used to infringe copyright.

Excuses Unlikely To Work

Each of the following may be a breach of copyright:

- Copying for personal enjoyment.

- Changing the material slightly to make it look different (eg rearranging the paragraphs, renaming the characters).

- Transforming it into a different type of work (eg taking a photograph of a sculpture).

- Claiming that you created your copy independently, without being able to show any trace of where "your" idea came from or how it evolved.

- Not taking any payment for the illicit copies you give to others.

- Copying only a large part or a small but crucial part instead of the whole work.

- Paying the author to create the work. Unless you agree with the author that you will own the copyright, this will give you a licence to use the work for the purposes for which it was created but will not entitle you to exploit the work in other ways nor will it necessarily allow you to licence others to use the work.

Elizabeth Barnett is a Solicitor at Corrs Chambers Westgarth © 1999.
She is based in Melbourne. http://www.ccw.com.au

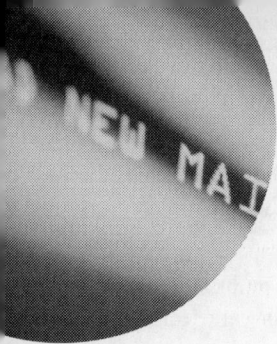

Australia's E-Transactions Bill – Where it's At

By Ann Slater

The Electronic Transactions Bill was passed by the Australian parliament late in 1999.

The bill attempts to facilitate a "technology-neutral" approach to the recognition of electronic transactions by deeming certain electronic communications to meet existing legal requirements for writing, signatures and the production and retention of documents.

More specifically, the bill:

- Defines an "electronic communication" to include data, text, images and speech which is processed at its destination by an automated voice recognition system;

- Covers both commercial and non-commercial transactions;

- Extends in its operation beyond communications with Commonwealth Government entities. If a non-government recipient of information consents to receiving information electronically, the legislation will apply;

- States that the requirements for providing a signature to a Commonwealth government entity will be met if the entity's information technology requirements are met;

- States that copyright will not be infringed by the generation or production of an electronic form of a document for the purposes of the legislation or corresponding state legislation; and

- Contemplates regulations being made to specify the form in which electronic copies of documents may be stored in order to satisfy document retention requirements.

The draft bill was released by the Commonwealth Government for public comment in January 1999 and was subject to considerable criticism by the industry and lawyers due to the vagueness of its light-handed and "technology neutral" approach.

The fact that the draft bill only applied to communications with Commonwealth government agencies was also a strong criticism of its effectiveness. At the time the draft bill was released, the Commonwealth Government stated that it intended that the states and territories would enact complementary legislation, to enable a federal framework to be established that would apply to all electronic transactions.

What Are the States Up To?

The only state to have taken any clear, positive action with respect to the bill is Victoria [*at the time of going to press – Editor*]. In December 1998, the Victorian Government released a draft of its own Electronic Commerce Framework Bill for public consultation.

When the draft bill was released, the Victorian Government stated that it intended to participate in the proposal for the national harmonisation of electronic transactions legislation in line with the Commonwealth's bill. However, the Victorian Government stated that it would not wait for such legislation to be drafted and debated and that it intended to enact its own legislation as an interim measure.

The Victorian Government indicated that it would amend its own legislation to fit in with the national model, after the Commonwealth legislation was enacted. The Electronic Commerce Framework Bill has not yet been released in final form or tabled in parliament.

The other states and territories have not made any clear indications recently of their progress or intentions with respect to electronic transactions legislation. At the end of the day, the Commonwealth may be wide enough in its operation to cover most electronic transactions in any event.

Ann Slater is a Partner at PricewaterhouseCoopers Legal, and specialises in Intellectual Property, Technology and Media. She is based in Sydney.
http://www.pwclegal.com.au

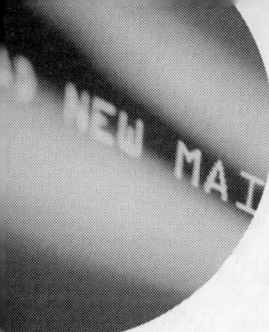

Electronic Transactions Bill 1999

The following is a simplified outline of the Act:
A Bill for an Act to facilitate electronic transactions and for other purposes

- For the purposes of a law of the Commonwealth, a transaction is not invalid because it took place by means of one or more electronic communications.

- The following requirements imposed under a law of the Commonwealth can be met in electronic form:

(a) a requirement to give information in writing;

(b) a requirement to provide a signature;

(c) a requirement to produce a document;

(d) a requirement to record information;

(e) a requirement to retain a document.

- For the purposes of a law of the Commonwealth, provision is made for determining the time and place of the dispatch and receipt of an electronic communication.

- The purported originator of an electronic communication is bound by it for the purposes of a law of the Commonwealth only if the communication was sent by the purported originator or with the authority of the purported originator.

On The Dotted Line – Digital Signatures

By Brendan Scott

P aper has served the human race well for thousands of years. But is it really still necessary to stand outside in the cold waiting for the taxi with the documents in order to strike a contract? The answer is, technically, no. One reason is digital signatures.

It is not necessary for someone to put pen to paper for there to be a binding contract. The law itself does not place any restrictions upon the manner in which a deal can be struck or even how that deal is evidenced. What the law looks for is the "objective" agreement that has been reached between the parties.

Forming a Contract

A contract can be formed verbally – "yep, that sounds fine to me", physically – nodding in agreement, or by practically any other means.

Traditionally, lawyers have resorted to making separate execution copies for every party to the agreement, with every party not only signing the agreement, but also initialling each page. In this situation, it is abundantly clear which documents constitute the agreement. If any page is lost or damaged, there is at least one other copy for reference. When the contract is signed, it is also usual for a third party to witness the signature and sign the document in confirmation. All of these methods and procedures ultimately make it very difficult (but not impossible) to dispute the fact of an agreement or its contents.

The Question of Identity

So, in using a digital signature, there are a number of hurdles to be overcome. You have to be able to prove the identity of the person applying the signature. Digital signatures in general have no "personality" as such – they're just numbers. Unlike a handwritten signature, they are not imbibed with any aspect of the person applying them. As such, it is easier for a rogue to assert that they are the person associated with the particular signature. This is where certification authorities come in. Certification authorities serve the purpose of verifying the identity of the person to whom a given signature belongs.

There are other issues associated with the use of digital secrecy – can the (electronic) document be admitted into evidence in court for example?

On the Privacy Front

There is also a whole can of worms on the privacy front. If all digital transactions can be linked to a specific person, retailers are able to build enormous, detailed profiles on a person's movements, habits and interests on a scale unheard of by older generations. What happens if the certification authority is in the private sector, rather than the public? Can they sell their lists? How do you store electronically signed documents? Are your archival procedures up to the task?

Suffice to say that before you rush out and get your lawyer to draw up an e-contract on which to test your new digital signature, you need to make sure they have at least a handle on what the issues are. Good luck.

Brendan Scott is a partner at law firm Gilbert & Tobin, specialising in ecommerce and the law of electronic document management. http://www.gtlaw.com.au

Sending Viruses Could Land You in Court

Sending virus-infected emails which cause outside computer systems to crash can land the sender in court, Michael Dodge, technology partner at Melbourne law firm, Arnold Bloch Leibler, warns.

So in order to limit the risk of liability for any damage they cause, businesses should "arm themselves with all the technology they can get", he says.

"Everyone is excited about e-commerce, people are not considering what they send," he adds. Companies should have the latest virus scanners and scan all emails that go out.

"Watch what you're sending and, if it looks dubious, don't send it." He says a disclaimer on emails telling receivers to virus scan the message before opening it could limit liability if the receiver did not follow the warning. But, ultimately, it will be a court's decision.

Companies whose computer systems crash because of emails could also sue their IT consultants for not providing adequate firewalls or software manufacturers because they failed to protect the systems, Dodge says.

There was little case law to indicate what would occur in cases of email negligence, he adds. The principle would be based on the "snail in the bottle" case, the landmark 1932 Donoghue v Stevenson case that established negligence law.

Dodge says in determining whether a person has been negligent, one has to ascertain whether the person owes a "duty of care" to the injured party and if so, whether the person took "reasonable care" to prevent the injury.

In order to succeed in an action against the sender of a virus-infected email, it has to be established that the sender owed a "duty of care" to the recipient. This duty can be established even if the parties are not in a commercial or professional relationship, as it is likely that a virus-infected email can cause damage to the recipient, he says.

"At the moment it's like the wild west ... everyone's doing their own thing. But, as soon as a problem develops, the sheriff will come into town ... it will be a shock to the system."

SOURCE: E-Commerce Today, Issue 10, September 3, 1998.
http://www.ecommercetoday.com.au

When Sending Staff Email Constitutes Piracy

A major threat to organisations is legal liability for bootlegged material emailed by staff. Pirated MP3 music files emailed around the office and beyond are exposing organisations to the risk of legal liability for copyright theft, according to internet content security specialist Content Technologies.

Content Technologies is warning companies that as the craze for downloading music from the internet increases, so do the numbers of pirated MP3 tracks being emailed around.

It also is advising companies to update and amend their corporate email policies to cover themselves against the risks of legal liability associated with MP3.

"MP3 technology is here to stay. It has even become the most widely searched-for term on the web," said Alan Schaverien, managing director of Content Technologies Asia-Pacific. "However, more and more people are making illegal copies of music and emailing them onto friends or colleagues. This work-time music could cost a great deal in legal repercussions if companies are not careful."

"If an employee downloads an illegally-copied MP3 track from the internet, that's a problem for the employee," said Brett Oaten, principal of Brett Oaten Solicitors, a leading Sydney-based entertainment law firm.

"But if an employee sends a bootlegged MP3 track via company email, the company is implicitly involved in the illegal distribution of copyright material," said Oaten. "That is a problem for the company".

"Artists regard the opportunity to distribute their material via the internet as an extremely exciting development," said Oaten, whose firm represents artists including silverchair, Human Nature and Wendy Matthews. "However, they intend to vigorously pursue anyone who does infringe their copyright via MP3 or any other technology."

"Nobody wants to put a stop to MP3, but companies need to protect themselves by keeping their eyes open and having clear email and Web access policies in place," Schaverien added.

"The fact that companies may be legally liable for bootlegged files is a very real issue. Companies need to be more aware of which web sites their employees are visiting, as well as what is being passed around by email, to protect themselves against potential risks."

Content Technologies is a developer of internet content security and policy management solutions. http://www.mimesweeper.com.au

The Perils of Ignoring Privacy

Introduction – Keeping the Customer Satisfied

Privacy concerns are the biggest stumbling block to doing business online. Effective, profitable customer and business relationships depend on confidence and trust. The right to private and secure electronic communications is of chief importance to your business, your customers and your employees.

Privacy is Good Business Practice

Privacy is good business sense and privacy concerns most email users.

Research conducted by Forrester Research in September 1999 and published in a report: "Privacy Best Practice Market Overview" found that two-thirds of web consumers had serious concerns about online privacy.

The report found that the more concerned that web users were, the less likely they were to want email from retailers, to participate in group email lists or to chat online. Web users were also likely to lie about their personal details online, due to concerns about avoiding junk email and about how the site would use the information. Forrester also found that consumers preferred to give out personal information when privacy was guaranteed.

Another piece of research carried out by AT&T and published in the article "What Net Users Want", offers an overview in this chapter summarises the personal privacy apprehensions of net users and details different levels of privacy concern.

Devising a Privacy Policy is Important

A privacy policy is now essential for any business that either asks for information about customers or has the ability to collect and store information about them. Without this kind of policy, the credibility of the business concerned is severely compromised.

The benefits to be earned by using privacy policies are addressed in "How Net Privacy can Boost e-Commerce", which offers a number of simple and cost-effective strategies to help online organisations to encourage consumers to submit personal information without compromising privacy.

A summary of the use of privacy policies on Australian business websites is the subject of a study and discussion article "Australia Slow on Privacy Uptake" by Rod Brooks.

Survey of Use of Email Lists

The chapter also addresses specific attitudes to privacy and email in a survey by ePrivacy, commissioned by *The Email for Business Handbook*. Some of Australia's most popular online organisations were surveyed on their use of email and email lists. The findings show that email is widely used for promotional purposes but that most organisations oppose the use of spam and are not prepared to transfer the information to a third party under any circumstances.

While most organisations were not fully aware of the current legal position relating to privacy or proposed legislation, the study found that all respondents agreed there was a moral obligation to inform the user of the purpose for which their personal information would be used.

Employee Privacy

Privacy is an issue of concern not only to customers. Email use in the workplace can lead to greater employee surveillance at work and is regarded as an invasion of privacy on the same level as reading snail mail or listening to phone calls. Or so says the Community & Public Sector Union's professional division in "Should Staff email be Checked?"

Then, in another article, "Policing and Protection at Work", the NSW Council for Civil Liberties argues that employers should be required under legislation to inform employees about the level of email protection in their workplace and whether email will be scanned or not.

For further discussion of email in the workplace and email policies, check articles in the chapter Managing Your Email.

What Net Users Want

By Lorrie Faith Cranor, Joseph Reagle and Mark S. Ackerman

P eople are concerned about privacy, particularly online. In order to better understand the nature of online privacy concerns, AT&T reported on 381 questionnaires completed in November 1998 by US internet users.

The aim was to look beyond the fact that people are concerned and attempt to understand how they are concerned.

The major findings of this research that can be related to the use of email and internet users' attitudes to providing their email address are:

• Internet users are more likely to provide information when they are not identified.

Respondents were much less willing to provide information when personally identifiable information was requested.

• Some types of data are more sensitive than others.

Respondents were generally comfortable providing preference details, for example on a favourite television program, however, they were often very uncomfortable providing credit card numbers.

There were also differences in sensitivity to seemingly similar kinds of data. Most respondents said they would never or rarely feel comfortable providing their phone number but would usually or always feel comfortable providing their email address. The comfort level for postal mail addresses fell somewhere in between.

Respondents were consistently less comfortable in allowing a child to provide information than in providing it themselves

• **Many factors are important in decisions about information disclosure.**

When deciding whether or not to provide information, respondents reported that the most important factor was whether or not information would be shared with other companies and organisations.

Other highly important factors included whether information would be used in an identifiable way, the kind of information collected and the purpose for which the information was collected.

Whether a site posts a privacy policy, whether a site has a privacy seal of approval and whether a site discloses a data retention policy were viewed as questions which were important, but less so than other factors.

• **Internet users dislike unsolicited communications.**

Respondents indicated a strong desire to avoid unsolicited communications.

Sixty-one percent of respondents, who said they would be willing to provide their name and postal mail address to a site in order to receive free pamphlets and coupons, said they would be less likely to provide the information if it was shared with other companies.

In written comments, as one respondent noted: "I already get too much junk mail." Others expressed concerns about unsolicited marketing: "I would not want to have telemarketers, email messages, direct mail, etc. coming as I get too much of that anyway" and "I don't mind receiving literature that I request, but I DO NOT like to receive unsolicited mail, email or phone calls."

While respondents indicated a clear dislike for unsolicited communications, they were less concerned (but not unconcerned) about unsolicited email. Respondents were more comfortable providing their email address than they were their postal address or their phone number. Furthermore, they expressed less concern about unsolicited email and about websites collecting email addresses for marketing lists than they did about websites collecting personal information from children, or someone tracking what websites people visit and using that information improperly.

• **Internet users dislike automatic data transfer.**

Most respondents do not want tools to transfer information about them to websites (cookies) automatically.

• **A joint program of privacy policies and privacy seals seemingly provides a comparable level of user confidence as that provided by privacy laws.**

> **TIP**
> When deciding whether to provide information, the most important factor to net users was whether the information would be shared with other organisations

How Concerned Are Internet Users About Privacy?

AT&T found that while most respondents were concerned about privacy, (only 13% said they were "not very" or "not at all" concerned about privacy threats), their reactions to scenarios involving online data collection were extremely varied. The research identified three groups with different levels of privacy concerns.

The Privacy Fundamentalists

These respondents were extremely concerned about any use of their data and generally unwilling to provide their data to websites, even when privacy protection measures were in place.

They were twice as likely as the other groups to report having been a victim of an invasion of privacy on the internet. About a third of the fundamentalists refused to answer questions about their household income (as compared with 14% of the pragmatists and 3% of the marginally concerned).

The Pragmatists

These respondents often had specific concerns and particular tactics for addressing them. For example, the concerns of pragmatists were often significantly reduced by the presence of privacy protection measures such as privacy laws or privacy policies on websites.

The Marginally Concerned

These respondents were generally willing to provide data to websites under almost any condition, although they often expressed a mild general concern about privacy. Nonetheless, under some conditions, the marginally concerned seemed to value their privacy. For example, they highly rated the ability to have themselves removed from marketing mailing lists.

Thus, AT&T reported that it seems unlikely that a one-size-fits-all approach to online privacy is likely to succeed.

A full version of this report 'Beyond Concern - Understanding Net Users' Attitudes About Online Privacy' is available at: http://www.research.att.com/projects/privacy study

Lorrie Faith Cranor is from AT&T Labs-Research, Joseph Reagle from the World Wide Web Consortium and the Massachusetts Institute of Technology and Mark S. Ackerman from the Information and Computer Science, University of California.

How Net Privacy Can Boost E-Commerce

By Ben Macklin

Privacy concerns are a considerable impediment to consumers engaging in electronic commerce. Research shows that most internet users are more than prepared to reveal personal information to online merchants, provided they receive some value in doing so. A recent study in the United States revealed that 86% of respondents felt that trading information for benefits was a fair exchange.

Apart from future legal requirements to inform users about information collection practices, there are a number of economic and strategic reasons why developing privacy initiatives for online organisations are particularly valuable. Building trust with the website visitor fosters a relationship that will encourage them to do three important things:

1. They will be more willing to return to your site;

2. They will be more willing to purchase a good or service from you; and

3. They will be more willing to submit personal information about what they want and need from you as a business.

All these elements can have a positive effect on your business bottom line.

Privacy initiatives can also enhance the corporate reputation of an e-business and make both consumers, regulators and privacy advocates aware of the importance privacy plays for the organisation.

The Value of Personal Information

Personal information will be the currency that drives business-to-consumer electronic commerce over the next few years. If an online organisation knows who their visitors and customers are, then they can tailor goods and services and personalise the content to meet their needs and wants, thereby efficiently allocating resources. This same consumer data can also provide advertisers with the most predictive information about the buying habits of current and potential customers. Such knowledge is understandably highly valued by advertisers. Those organisations which collect such data will be in a position to attract more advertisers and charge a higher rate for the space they provide. The ability to analyse and respond to consumer data will become a value differentiator between those online organisations that survive and those that make a profit. In order to gather this data, however, consumers must be able to trust the organisation with their information.

TIP

If sites post and follow good privacy policies, consumers will come, carrying personal information. Violate the promises and they will leave

Privacy Policies Do Matter

Survey results reveal that most net users are more willing to reveal personal information if the website displays a comprehensive privacy policy which clearly explains what personal information is being collected and how the organisation is using it. As privacy expert Alan Westin explains: "If sites post and follow good privacy policies, consumers will come, carrying personal information. Violate the promises and they will leave."

Some Privacy Strategies

There are a number of simple and cost-effective strategies that will help online organisations encourage consumers submit personal information without compromising privacy.

- Develop a privacy policy for your website that lets the consumer know what you are doing with their personal information and adhere to it.

- If you use cookies, let consumers know about it and what the purpose is. Try not to restrict services if consumers do not want to receive cookies.

- Allow the consumer to "opt-in" to email marketing (consensual marketing) as well as the ability to easily "opt-out" if they so wish. Compared to the average click-through rate of 0.65% for banner ads, opt-in email marketing has an average response rate of between 15-40%. It is a very effective means of online marketing!

- Do not restrict services to visitors if they do not wish to submit personal information. They will simply leave and never come back. In fact, give consumers an opportunity to use all your services anonymously if they so wish.

- Offer a secure payment system that requires the consumer to only submit personal information that is necessary for the transaction to take place. Offer alternative payment systems such as BPAY and Cybercash if possible.

- If you want to extract personal information from the consumer, give them something in return. Offer a prize, a discount or "premiere" membership if they are prepared to submit detailed personal information.

- Let consumers know who you are, (a photo sometimes helps) and how they can contact you.

- Be aware that consumers are concerned about their privacy.

Extracted from 'The Commercial Value of Privacy Initiatives', by Ben Macklin, Director of ePrivacy. http://www.eprivacy.com.au

Australia Slow on the Uptake of Privacy Policies

According to a 1998 *BusinessWeek* survey, privacy was found to be the number one consumer issue facing the internet – of more concern than cost, ease of use, security or spam. Some people believe that concerns about lack of privacy are slowing the growth of e-commerce. So, which Australian websites have privacy policies?

In a survey of the 50 Australian websites most accessed by Australians (from http://usrwww.mpx.com.au/~ianw/) only 20% mention anything about privacy. And some of these privacy statements could more correctly be described as non-privacy policies.

A survey conducted in April 1999 by Australian Business Advisers found that very few Australian corporate and consumer websites have privacy policies.

The survey of Australia's top 100 companies (by market capitalisation) showed that only 5% of the 79 companies that have a website have an online privacy policy.

Amazingly, only 6% of the 129 websites surveyed by Australian Business Advisers promised not to disclose any personal information. Eighty-eight percent of sites failed to mention anything about what they would do with information collected from users. And 5% of websites stated that any and all information collected was deemed to be non-confidential and could be used in any way they chose, including disclosure to others "without limitation".

Many companies need to wake up. Online privacy concerns are real and need to be addressed. Websites should tell people what information is being collected, how it will be used, what choices are available regarding the collection, use and distribution of their information, the security procedures in place to protect users' collected information from loss, misuse or alteration and how users can update or correct inaccuracies in their information.

For most companies, the lack of a privacy policy is more likely to be due to not seeing it as a priority rather than anything sinister, but people should have some concerns about the use of information statements on a number of websites.

One top 100 company has the following quote in its copyright, trademarks and disclaimer section:

"Any information, ideas, concepts, know-how or technologies provided by or obtained from you or your use of [named company's] website shall be deemed to be non-confidential and [named company] shall be free to reproduce, use, disclose and distribute the information to others without limitation."

Whilst some of these conditions may be designed to protect the company from breach of copyright suits by people claiming to have given them commercial ideas over the internet, there is no mention of the exclusion of personal information. As this site allows the payment of bills by credit card, does this mean they can share the credit card information with anyone?

Similarly, a number of very popular websites have the same Terms of Use, which includes the following quote:

"[Named company] and its affiliates may gather, process and use (and allow others to use): a) the information which you submit or otherwise provide when using the network (including your name, physical address, email address and any other details you provide), b) information regarding the manner in which you use the network (including without limitation all information gathered as a result of the use of "cookies"). From time to time, [named company] may offer and may allow others to offer products and services to you. If you wish to discontinue receiving such offers, please contact as appropriate [named company] or the relevant affiliate."

As this information is not prominently displayed where people provide this sort of personal information, I wonder how many people realise that their personal details can be disclosed to others?

A good privacy policy should provide contact details for exactly who to contact to opt out.

Many websites ask for personal details for any query or even for feedback. Often this information is optional, but rarely is the question of choice revealed. These sites should disclose how this information will be used. Only three websites were found to disclose what information is being collected and how it will be used –

www.newscorp.com.au, www.yahoo.com.au and www.altavista.yellowpages.com.au. Five sites had less comprehensive privacy policies which explained in detail either what is being collected, or how it will be used, but not both – www.aristocrat.com.au, www.bankwest.com.au, www.battleofthesexes.com.au, www.start.com.au and www.tradingpost.com.au. Seven sites said that any information provided was not confidential and could be disclosed to others.

Privacy has become such a big issue that IBM withholds advertising dollars from North American sites that do not post privacy policies. IBM estimates that just 30% of the 780 websites on which it advertises worldwide display a privacy statement. The USA Direct Marketing Association will deny membership to any company that does not comply with its privacy pledge. This includes posting privacy statements on websites. And Microsoft and TRUSTe are developing a Privacy Wizard to simplify the process of implementing an online privacy policy (see http://privacy.linkexchange.com).

Speeding up the crucial processes of enabling users to set their own privacy boundaries and letting sites post privacy policies is critical to helping e-commerce grow and heading off government regulation, according to Tara Lemmey, president and executive director of the Electronic Frontier Foundation.

So Australian websites have a responsibility to quickly develop, post and implement privacy policies.

Rod Brooks is a senior consultant with Australian Business Advisers, a Victorian based consultancy company. http://www.abaconsulting.com.au

OECD Adopts Privacy Declaration

I t makes "good business sense" for businesses to build relationships of trust with customers by respecting their personal information, as customers fully participate in the marketplace when they trust institutional infrastructure, Australia's privacy commissioner, Moira Scollay, told an OECD ministerial conference on e-commerce in 1998.

Users of e-commerce and the internet should have the right to be anonymous and, where that was not practical, transactions should be secure, she said.

Scollay was commenting after OECD ministerial representatives agreed on a privacy declaration to encourage countries and companies to adopt privacy policies to protect consumer rights. In taking a non-interventionist approach to privacy issues, the representatives agreed to "encourage" the adoption of privacy policies "whether implemented by legal, self-regulatory, administrative or technological means" and "encourage" the online notification of privacy policies to users. They also agreed to "encourage" the use of privacy enhancing technologies, promote awareness of privacy issues, and ensure "effective enforcement mechanisms are available" to address non-compliance with privacy principles.

Scollay said tools such as privacy enhancing technologies, online contracts, education and international agreements all played a role.

A mix of law and self-regulation was the most appropriate way to protect privacy.

SOURCE: E-Commerce Today, Issue 16, October 15, 1998.
http://www.ecommercetoday.com.au

Guidelines for Goodwill

By Australian Privacy Commissioner

The Australian Privacy Commissioner has released draft guidelines on workplace email, internet browsing and privacy. The guidelines comply with the Privacy Act 1988, which covers public sector employees. The commissioner hopes the private sector will adopt the guidelines as good privacy practice.

Email Laws

As the commissioner receives many inquiries regarding the privacy of workplace email, the commissioner's office said it was apparent there was a general expectation by staff that a law exists which protects their privacy in the workplace.

There is no general constitutional or common law right to privacy in Australia. However, the Federal Government intends to introduce "light touch" privacy legislation to cover the private sector, based on National Privacy Principles for the Fair Handling of Personal Information.

It is expected that the legislation will apply to staff emails that contain personal information, excluding "personnel records". The private sector legislation may also apply to the logs of staff web browsing activities.

The Guidelines

The guidelines are provided to assist organisations to develop policies or improve their existing policies.

1. A policy should be promulgated to staff and management should ensure that it is known and understood by staff. Ideally, the policy should be linked from a screen that the user sees when they log onto the network. Consultation with staff may also be useful. A consultative process can engender an understanding by management of the sorts of legitimate activities for which staff are using email and web browsing and increase the understanding by staff of the possible risk to the organisation associated with improper email and internet use.

2. The policy should be explicit about which activities are permitted and forbidden. While it is the prerogative of each organisation to determine what it considers to be appropriate usage of its system, to simply say that all activity must be "work-related" may not be clear. There may be scope for guidelines outlining what is "personal" use of email, both within the organisation and externally, to other organisations, as appropriate. Other activities may be specifically prohibited, eg. the use of email to harass, "flame" (to send abusive email) defame or disclose information or transmit pornography.

The issue of appropriate usage may be harder to define in respect to web browsing. It may not be possible to tell if a web page is relevant until it has been read. The operation of web search engines can result in surprising and irrelevant search results. Links on websites may also be misleading. Discussion with staff on the issue of work-related web use might help to clarify this issue. Where an organisation determines that usage is to be work-related only, it should clearly spell out what it considers to be work-related and not work-related. The policy should refer to any relevant legislation. In the Commonwealth public sector, this includes the Privacy Act, the Archives Act, the Freedom of Information Act, the Crimes Act, the Australian Public Service (APS) Code of Conduct, the Public Service Act and Regulations. APS Regulation 7(8) provides that employees "must use Commonwealth resources in a proper manner" and Regulation 7(11) requires employees to "behave in a way that upholds the APS values and the integrity and good reputation of the APS".

The Sex, Race and Disability Discrimination Acts and workplace relations law apply in both the public and private sectors. In particular, employers (please refer to the "Employers' Page on the Human Rights and Equal Opportunity Commission website".) should be aware of their obligations under these acts to protect employees against sexual harassment and racial vilification and other forms of unlawful discrimination which could occur through email and internet use. There may also be relevant state and territory statutes.

3. The policy should clearly set out what information is logged and who in the organisation has rights to access the logs and content of staff email and browsing activities. Staff email boxes will normally contain the emails they have sent and received. Back-ups and archives may also contain copies of emails that have been deleted by the user. As well as the actual content of messages, the date and time the message was transmitted, received and opened and the email addresses of the sender and recipients will normally be recorded. With web browsing, the URLs (Uniform Resource Locaters or website addresses) of sites visited, the dates and times they were visited and the duration of site visits may be logged. Normally, access rights to staff mail boxes and logs would be restricted to those with the responsibility for administering the system. Such access should be as limited as possible and the question of who has access rights should be clearly set out in the policy. The policy should outline in what circumstances IT staff can legitimately access staff emails and browsing logs. The policy should also indicate, in general terms, under what circumstances an organisation will disclose the contents of emails and logs. Many organisations will only do this on the production of a legal authority.

4. The policy should refer to the organisation's computer security policy. The improper use of email may pose a threat to system security, the privacy of staff and others and the legal liability of the organisation.

5. The policy should be reviewed on a regular basis in order to keep up with the accelerating development of the internet and information technology. The policy should be re-issued whenever significant change is made. This will help to reinforce the message to staff.

The Draft Guidelines on Workplace Email, Web Browsing and Privacy are designed to aid the development of clear policies in organisations in both the public and private sectors. A draft discussion paper can be viewed at: http://www.privacy.gov.au/issues/p7_4.html

Case Study: GeoCities Ordered to Divulge Data

A US out-of-court settlement in September 1998 highlighted the need for businesses to inform customers if they intend to use personal data which they have collected via their website for commercial purposes.

What Happened?

GeoCities, the operator of one of the internet's most popular websites, agreed to settle charges by the US Federal Trade Commission (FTC) that it breached trade practices law and misled consumers in obtaining and using personal identifying information.

A draft FTC consent order required GeoCities to implement procedures to inform customers about the purpose of the personal data collection and the likelihood of disclosure to third parties.

Among the charges GeoCities agreed to settle were that it falsely indicated that personal data would only be used for special offers and specifically requested products and services and that information would not be disclosed to third parties.

What Does That Mean to My Business?

IT lawyer Anne-Marie Allgrove, a senior associate with Baker & Mackenzie, Sydney, said the case means it is important for business to put privacy statements on their website. If they don't have a site, they should be careful "not to use the information in such a way that is contrary to customers' expectations".

Allgrove said the case is "a timely reminder" that Australian businesses trading or collecting information on the internet need to be careful not to use information in a way which is, or is likely to be misleading or deceptive.

Provisions in Australia's Trade Practices Act prohibiting misleading conduct are "arguably broader" than those in the US Federal Trade Commission Act, which GeoCities was alleged to have breached, Allgrove said.

She said businesses seeking to alleviate customer data privacy concerns by putting privacy statements on their site need to ensure that any such statements are accurate, complete, prominent and clear.

SOURCE: E-Commerce Today, Issue 11, September 10, 1998.
http://www.ecommercetoday.com.au

Call for Customer Contracts

B usinesses trading online should form privacy contracts with customers and appoint an independent enforcer if they want to inspire consumer trust, according to US President Bill Clinton's former senior internet adviser. The greatest resistance people had to trading online was a "fear that their privacy will somehow be compromised", Ira Magaziner told a conference in 1998.

"A seller should notify a buyer when they are collecting information and what they are going to use it for," he said. "The buyer should have the ability to say 'no, that I don't want to do business on that basis. Or the buyer should have the ability to say 'I'll give you that information, but only if you use it this way and not that way'."

Once the relationship is established, Magaziner suggests there should be some form of independent enforcement of that contract, as outlined in the OECD's privacy protection guidelines. The OECD privacy guidelines are at: www.oecd.org//dsti/sti/it/secur/prod/priv-en.htm

These could include:

- The display of a seal on a website from a privacy body such as the Online Privacy Alliance (www.privacyalliance.org)

- An audit by an independent body

- A consumer redress mechanism for consumers to seek redress with a third party and request adjudication in cases of dispute

"The principle of empowering consumers to protect themselves is a fundamental principle of the internet age," Magaziner said.

A survey released in January 1998 by US-based research firm Cheskin Research and website interface design firm Studio Archetype/Sapient also concluded that brand, navigation ease, order fulfilment, presentation, up-to-date technology and the logos of security-guaranteeing firms were the essential characteristics of websites to communicate trustworthiness to visitors.

The eCommerce Trust Study (www.studioarchetype.com/cheskin) concluded that in order to address privacy (and security) concerns, online traders could "clearly state their policies on security and encryption, ask for only necessary information, provide shipping and return guarantees and provide good communication with consumers".

SOURCE: E-Commerce Today, Issue 40, April 29, 1999.
http://www.ecommercetoday.com.au

Policing and Privacy Protection at Work

By Kevin O'Rourke

The NSW Council for Civil Liberties is concerned about the lack of a privacy framework for email in the workplace. In Australia, there is no constitutional protection of privacy, no common law right to privacy and only limited statutory protection covering tax file numbers and the like.

What Should the Law Do?

There are laws prohibiting the opening of mail delivered through the postal system and most employers would not think of opening a letter to an employee marked "private and confidential". There are also laws prohibiting the use of a listening device to listen to a telephone conversation, though these do not affect the monitoring of calls in a direct marketing context.

Employees Dismissed

In 1999, two council employees in NSW were dismissed for the "inappropriate" use of email in the workplace. The emails were "personal" messages to each other. The letters of dismissal attached copies of all their messages to each other, in which they referred to their bosses as Huey, Dewey and Louis.

The NSW Council for Civil Liberties has been approached by several IT managers who have been instructed by employers to print all email messages of particular employees. The IT managers have uniformly expressed concern about what they have been asked to do and most are seeking advice about whether they are breaking any laws.

We are also aware that some employers are using scanning software to search all emails for keywords. The keywords often include the names of senior management, who are keen to discover what employees "privately" think about them.

The Right to Know

The NSW Council for Civil Liberties is currently lobbying for legislation to protect private email communications in the workplace. In our opinion, employers should, as a minimum, be required to inform employees about the level of email protection in their workplace and, in particular, whether email will be scanned or otherwise dealt with.

This is analogous to recent (1999) legislation covering video surveillance in the workplace. In broad terms, employers must inform employees if they are to be the subject of video surveillance. If the video surveillance is to be done in secret (for example, the employer has reasonable grounds to suspect that a particular employee is stealing), a warrant must be obtained.

In the interim, while we await such legislation covering email, the NSW Council for Civil Liberties is encouraging employers to inform employees of their email policy. At the very least, this will avoid employees making false assumptions about the privacy of email messages.

Whatever the state of the law, it should not be forgotten that privacy, once famously described as the right to be let alone, is a fundamental human right. To invade the privacy of an individual is to lower the dignity and worth of that person, which is hardly conducive to good workplace relations.

Extracted from "Protecting Privacy and Employees In The Workplace", by Kevin O'Rourke, president of the NSW Council for Civil Liberties.
http://people.enternet.com.au/~cclnsw/

Should Staff Email be Checked?

Email leads to greater employee surveillance at work but is as much an invasion of privacy as reading snail mail or listening to phone calls, says Joanna Mullins, Community & Public Sector Union, professional division, assistant secretary.

Workplace privacy invasions, including the undetectable interception of email, checking documents held electronically and monitoring phone call lengths through sophisticated billing systems are not widespread in Australia yet, but the potential is there.

The NSW Labour Council has also asked the NSW Government to regulate what it says is the "unfettered rights of employers" to eavesdrop on employees' emails. Secretary Michael Costa said the practice is an "emerging issue" and is "open to abuse".

Surveillance has seen some employers crack down on email and web use. Many government employees, for example, are not allowed to email or surf the net for personal purposes and one particular overseas company intercepts all email, rejecting messages containing "forbidden words". Mullins says electronic surveillance is "more a control issue than anything else. If employers do not consider it appropriate to screen employees' personal mail, listen to their telephone calls and private conversations or periodically go through their filing cabinets and desks to see what's there, why should this be accepted electronically?" Mullins suggests it's a waste of time for most employers anyway. "Is there any point in surveying all staff, when 98% of staff will do well?"

SOURCE: E-Commerce Today, Issue 21, November 19, 1998.
http://www.ecommercetoday.com.au

Our Own Survey of Email Use in Australia

I n September 1999, ePrivacy was commissioned by *E-Commerce Today* to do a small survey of some of Australia's most popular online organisations and their use of email and email lists. The purpose of the pilot survey was to obtain a snapshot of the use of email and email lists by some of Australia's most popular online organisations. While the sample is too small to draw substantive conclusions, it does provide valuable insight into online practices by these organisations and indicates the need for further research into the area, in the lead-up to the introduction of proposed privacy legislation.

Key Findings

While it would be perilous to draw any substantive conclusions before further study is conducted, if the sample of responses is reflective of the wider online community, then most online organisations are at least aware of the privacy concerns that many consumers feel when using the internet. The use of email is widely used for promotional purposes, but most organisations are not prepared to transfer this information to a third party under any circumstances and do not condone the use of spam. While most organisations may not be fully aware of the current legal position relating to privacy or the government's proposed legislative scheme, all respondents indicated at least a moral obligation to inform the user of the purpose of collecting personal information.

Q1. Has your organisation or will it in the future use email addresses that users submit or that you request from them, for marketing or promotional purposes?

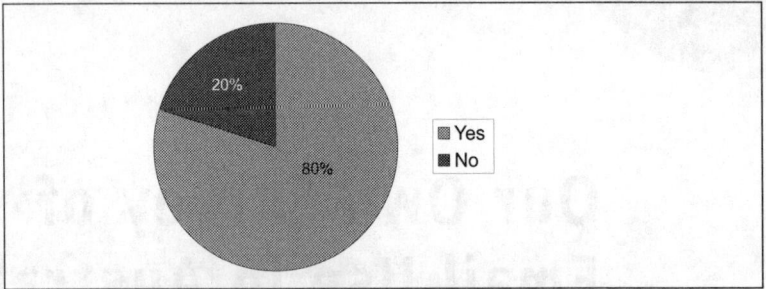

It seems clear from the results that the overwhelming percentage of organisations use email as a marketing or promotional tool. Considering that email as a promotional tool is a cheap and effective medium, it seems surprising that some online organisations are not using it.

Q2. Has your organisation or would your organisation in the future be prepared to purchase an email list or direct marketing list if it was offered to you?

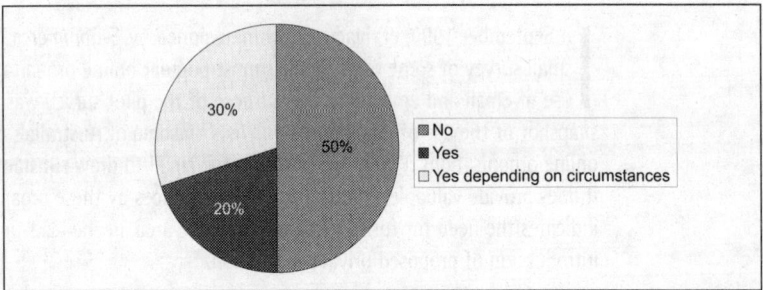

Q3. Has your organisation or would your organisation in the future be prepared to sell your email list or customer information to another organisation if the price was right?

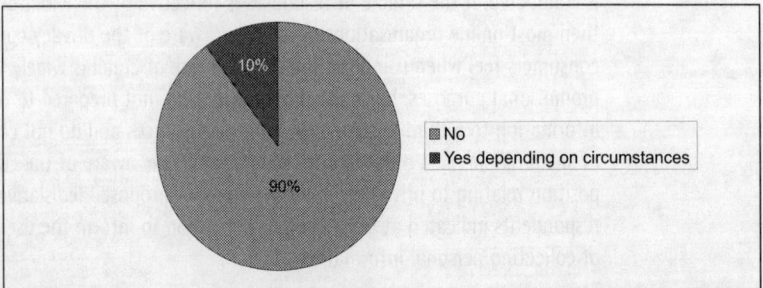

Most organisations would not purchase an email or direct marketing list, but some would consider it if the quality of the list was good and they were assured that email recipients had "opted-in". Most organisations would not sell their email list to a third party.

Q4. Would it be an economic hindrance for your organisation to give consumers the option of "opting-in" to direct marketing, rather than having them "opt-out"?

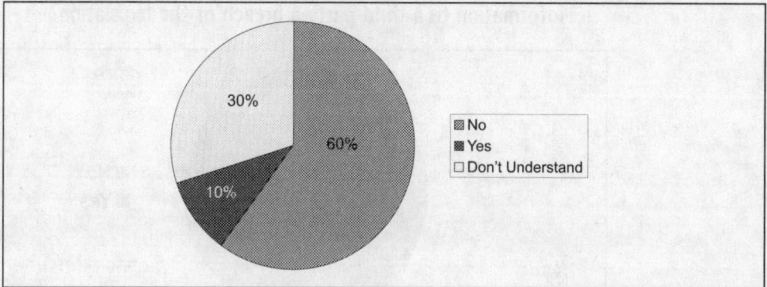

The government is in the process of introducing privacy legislation for the private sector that will allow organisations to use personal information for a purpose other than for the purpose of collection (a secondary purpose) if it is for the purpose of direct marketing. This means that organisations will be allowed to send unsolicited commercial email (spam) as long as they allow the individual to "opt-out" of any further direct marketing. The purpose of question four was to gauge whether it would be an economic hindrance for organisations to allow the consumer to "opt-in" instead of having them "opt-out". (This question was possibly a little confusing, as some respondents indicated they did not understand.) The results indicate that of those that understood the question, it would not put any undue economic burden on them to allow consumers to make the choice of whether or not they received direct marketing. One respondent indicated, however, that there were some technical issues in allowing consumers to completely "opt-in".

Q5. Do you feel it necessary to inform the user of the purpose for which the personal information you collect is used?

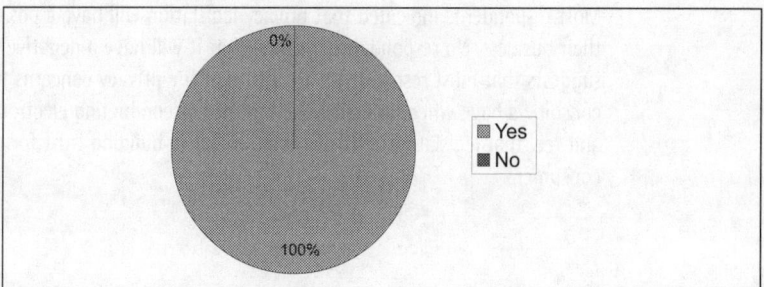

All organisations indicated that the user should be informed of the purpose for which the information is collected and used. Unfortunately, not all of these organisations backed this up with a comprehensive privacy statement on their website that indicates what information is collected and how it is to be used.

Q6. Are you aware that the government is in the process of introducing privacy legislation for the private sector that will make the transfer of personal information to a third party a breach of the legislation?

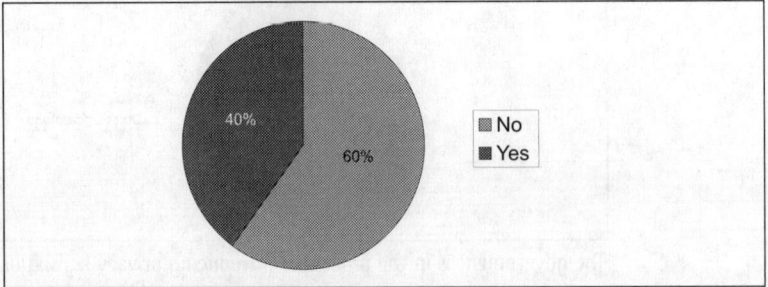

Most respondents indicated they were not aware of the government's proposed privacy legislation. No doubt once the legislation is written and released for public comment, this percentage will increase.

Q7. Can you foresee privacy legislation having a positive or negative effect on your business?

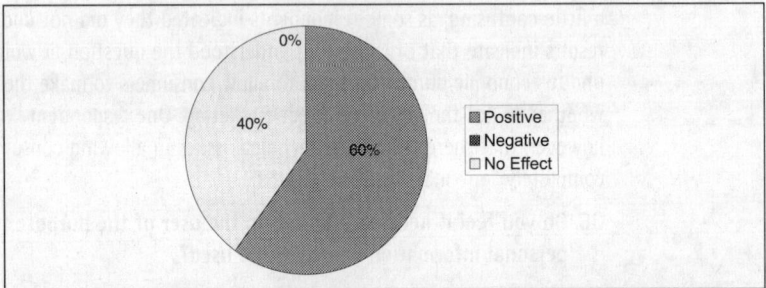

Most respondents indicated that privacy legislation will have a positive effect on their business. No respondent indicated that it will have a negative effect. This suggests that most respondents are aware of the privacy concerns that many consumers have when accessing the internet or conducting electronic commerce and feel that legislation will have some effect in building trust for the online consumer.

Q8. Do you feel your organisation has the right to do what it likes with the personal information a user submits to your organisation?

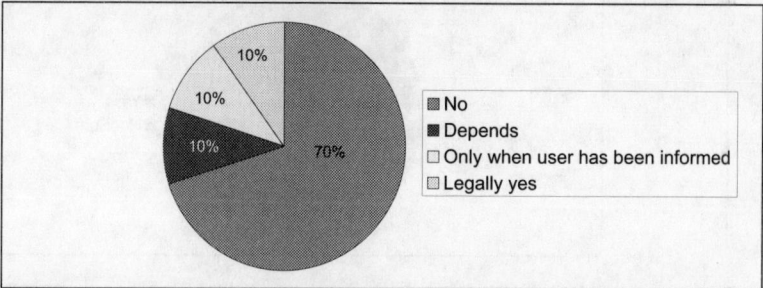

Most respondents indicated that they did not have any right to do what they liked with the personal information a user submits. While most respondents probably saw this as a moral issue, there is currently nothing to legally prevent organisations from selling personal information to a third party, from using it for direct marketing or any other purpose for that matter.

Q9. Do you think individual consumers should be able to charge organisations for the personal information the organisation uses? For example if you want my email address or postal address you can have it for 10 cents.

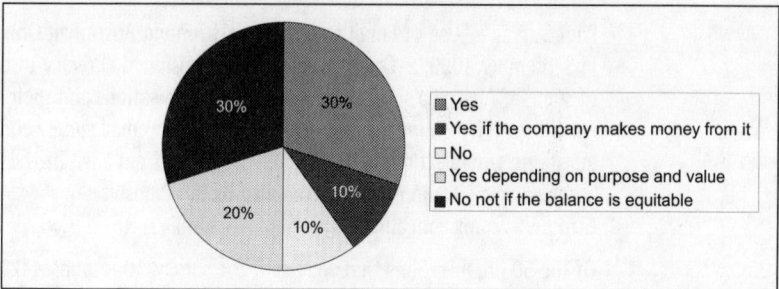

Speculation has arisen in Australia and overseas about whether consumers can charge for divulging their personal information to organisations. The argument goes that since organisations reap considerable value from the personal information a consumer submits, the individual should be able to charge. There was a mixed response from respondents. Most argued that as long as there was an equitable exchange (e.g. better service) between the consumer and merchant then there would be no need for a financial exchange.

Q10. Should unsolicited commercial email (spam) be outlawed?

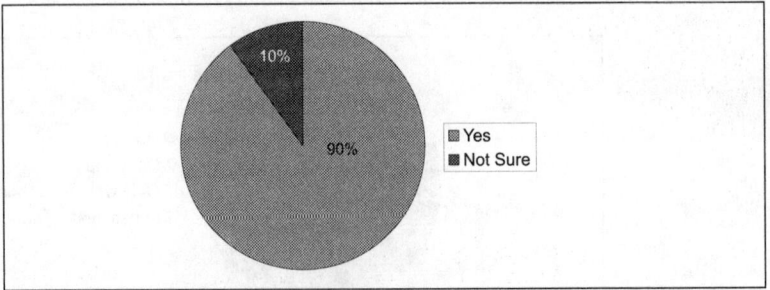

Most respondents indicated that they thought unsolicited commercial email (spam) should be outlawed. There is currently nothing to legally prevent organisations from sending spam, although most internet service providers and email services have a policy on it. Nor is there any provision within the proposed privacy legislation that will prevent spam.

A comment from one respondent is worth repeating: "Spam indicates a lack of understanding of the true value of a relationship with a customer."

About the Survey

Pilot Survey – "Use of Email and Email Lists Among Australian Online Organisations." In September 1999, *E-Commerce Today* commissioned ePrivacy to do a small survey of some of Australia's most popular online organisations and their use of email and email lists. Fifty online organisations were sent an email survey consisting of ten questions. Organisations were selected randomly from a list of the 100 most accessed web sites in Australia compiled by Ian Webster http://www.mpx.com.au/57Eianw/Sep99au.html.

Of the 50 organisations that were sent the survey, 10 responses (20%) were received. Organisations which responded included: RSVP (Manager), NineMSN (Marketing Manager), Seek (Editor), START (Marketing Manager), Wine Planet (e-publisher), JobNet (Marketing Manager), PinkBoard (Manager), Channel [v] (Online Manager), Travel.com.au (eMarketing Manager) and News Interactive (Marketing Manager).

Public Sector Privacy Laws

The first state legislation introduced in Australia to enforce email privacy rights requires NSW government departments and agencies to develop privacy management plans and public officials who divulge personal information or data about others may face jail and fines under data protection legislation.

The NSW Privacy and Data Protection Bill only extends to the public sector, because federal uniform laws will be needed for the private sector to operate efficiently, according to NSW attorney-general Jeff Shaw. The bill gives statutory recognition to specified data protection principles with which departments and agencies must comply.

Officials who corruptly disclose personal data about others face up to two years jail and fines of up to $11,000.

People whose personal data has been divulged by a government agency will also be eligible for $40,000 compensation. They can complain to the privacy commissioner, who can conciliate complaints but not enforce decisions. Complainants can instead choose to have a complaint reviewed by the agency concerned. A decision can then be reviewed by the Administrative Appeals Tribunal, which can make enforceable orders.

The term **personal information** is defined as: "information or an opinion, including information or an opinion forming part of a database, about an individual whose identity is apparent or can reasonably be ascertained".

Introducing the bill into state parliament, Shaw said evolving technologies made more detailed and extensive data protection measures necessary.

SOURCE: E-Commerce Today, Issue 14, October, 1998.
http://www.ecommercetoday.com.au

References

NSW Privacy Commissioner

The role of **Privacy NSW** is to promote and protect the right to privacy by advising individuals, government agencies and business organisations on what action they can take to protect the right to privacy, researching significant development in policy, law and technology which have an impact on privacy and making reports and recommendations to relevant authorities, investigating and where possible conciliating complaints about breaches of privacy, and answering enquiries and educating the community about privacy issues:
http://www.lawlink.nsw.gov.au/pc.nsf/pages/index

Electronic Frontiers Australia is dedicated to protection and promotion of the civil liberties of users and operators of computer based communications systems:
http://www.efa.org.au/

The eCommerce Trust Study is located at http://www.studioarchetype.com/cheskin

Recommendations Of The OECD Concerning Guidelines Governing The Protection Of Privacy And Transborder Flows Of Personal Data are located at
http://www.oecd.org//dsti/sti/it/secur/prod/priv-en.htm

For survey information regarding consumer privacy concerns, see Westin, Alan F, "Personal data 'freebies'... is this a fair bargain?", Computer World,
http://www.computerworld.com/home/print.nsf/all/990913C066 and
http://cyberatlas.internet.com/markets/retailing/ and
http://www.jup.com/jupiter/press/releases/1999/0817.html

Forrester Research has a wealth of material on the value of consumer data, consensual marketing and the value of privacy initiatives. http://www.forrester.com

For examples of good Australian privacy policies see Seek (www.seek.com.au) the ABC site (http://www.abc.net.au) or Yahoo Australia (http://www.yahoo.com.au)

Consumers Are Concerned About Personal Information

Forrester Technographics, a division of Forrester Research, carried out a survey, The Privacy Best Practice Market Overview, published in September 1999, of 10,000 North American online households.

Figures 1-1 and 1-2 show that most consumers are very concerned about releasing information online and that of these, 53% of the most experienced net users still worry about their privacy, indicating that fears do not decrease over time.

Figure 1-1: Consumers are concerned about releasing personal information online

Extremely/very concerned	67%
Somewhat concerned	24%
Not very/not at all concerned	9%

Figure 1-2: Time online barely eases consumer concerns

YEARS ONLINE	% OF CONSUMERS CONCERNED
0-1 years	76%
1-2 years	68%
2-3 years	68%
3-4 years	65%
4 + years	53%

SOURCE: Forrester Research, 1999 ©.

Protecting the Royal (e)Mail

Introduction

As the use of email grows exponentially every year, so do the risks of using it. Businesses and individuals the world over are eagerly embracing the speed, cost-effectiveness and efficiency of this new messaging technology but, unfortunately, it exposes businesses to the risks of viruses and interception.

However, there are solutions to these problems, in the form of encryption methods, digital signatures and other common sense daily security procedures.

Why does email need to be secure? Email is now a commonly-used tool, yet many business users have little idea how messages are sent or delivered. As an article in this chapter explains, there are methods on how to choose the right strength of security for email, how to make sure a standard protocol is being used and how to select security appropriate for e-commerce.

Changing passwords often and ensuring that spam is never responded to are some of the common sense ways that can be used to combat the risk of prying eyes. Companies can become familiar with stopping problems before they start through the use of policy and staff training, as another article in this chapter explains.

Other threats include unauthorised email copying, snooping and forgery which can all lead to loss of information, time, money and business reputation.

The risks are particularly significant when preventable viruses and their effects are considered. A case study in this issue reveals how the South Australian state government dealt with the Melissa virus which paralysed its internal mail system.

A 1999 Virus Prevalence Survey carried out by the International Computer Security Association found that 43% of surveyed companies had experienced a virus attack and that the cost of remedies ranged from over $5,000 to $100,000.

The details of the survey are discussed later in the chapter and, as Rob McMillan from the Australian Computer Emergency Response Team says in his article, the risks of virus infection are real and growing, with thousands of viruses out there on the web.

Some recommendations for virus prevention are keeping email server and client software up-to-date, ensuring that a modern firewall is in place (along with a proxy server) and using effective and up-to-date anti-virus software.

Encryption is one of the most effective preventative against unwanted attacks on email security. Yet the process is little understood, and has the aura of being the secret preserve of the techno gurus. Despite this, some big corporates such as banks and telcos have already adopted encryption. But the question remains for the encryption have-nots - where does one find encryption products and how exactly do they work?

The Information and Privacy Commissioner of Ontario, Canada, demystifies the concept and explains in this chapter how encryption works and what different methods are available, ranging from web-based encryption services to PC-based applications installed on a user's PC or network to public key infrastructures.

And for the diehards who only trust the fax machine and regard it as safer than any risky computer-based means of communication, the article "Why Faxes Are Not Secure", by Jim Heath of Viacorp, torpedoes the myth that faxes are safer by pointing out the obvious security problems.

The increasing importance being placed by business on email security is evident by recent research, reported also in this chapter, and by the rise in security software products – and other security measures like insurance.

Such insurance can also cover users for areas such as breach of confidentiality, defamation and infringement of intellectual property.

Defending Your Business From Virus Attacks

By Rob McMillan

Viruses have been around for many years. Strictly speaking, viruses are one category of attack programs. Other categories are trojan horses and worms. The noteworthy point about viruses is their ability to replicate and this is one of the reasons why they can be dangerous. Viruses can also be subcategorised – viruses may exist as part of another program (similar to a trojan horse), as a discrete program or more recently as a macro routine used in a widely-used application (as was the case with Melissa).

Virus Attacks on PCs

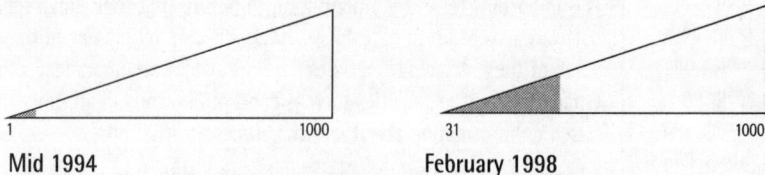

1 1000	31 1000
Mid 1994	February 1998

"The likelihood of a medium or large North American organisation having a virus encounter grew from about one encounter per 1,000 PCs per month in mid 1994 to about 31 chances per 1,000 PCs per month in February 1998".

For the purposes of the end user, however, the real goal is to avoid being a victim. The risk of infection is real. The internet is a network of over 50 million systems (as at July 1999). This represents a significant number of people, some of whom may have an interest in launching email-based attacks. The ICSA 1998 Computer Virus

Prevalence Survey found that "the likelihood of a medium or large North American organisation having a virus encounter grew from about one encounter per 1,000 PCs per month in mid-1994 to about 31 chances per 1,000 PCs per month in February, 1998". At that time, the internet was half the size it is now.

Viruses can be transferred in a number of ways besides email. Transfer via file downloads from the internet and physical distribution (ie floppy disks and CDs) have also been traditional favourites. There have been incidents in previous years where distribution media for widely-used programs have contained viruses.

In addition, a number of hoaxes have occurred in recent years. The US Department of Energy's CIAC team has an excellent online publication about these problems at http://ciac.llnl.gov/ciac/CIACHoaxes.html

Technically, viruses and related classes of tools may do some or all of the following – remove data on local and other network-connected systems, modify data, monitor data and disable a system or network either through a denial of service or destructive attack. But there are also social and business implications. These types of attack can inspire a lack of confidence in technology, either on the part of management or customer. This may translate into lost business opportunities as competitors forge ahead.

Likewise, attacks which indiscriminately send out arbitrary documents may result in commercial-in-confidence information reaching inappropriate eyes, thus leading to negative competition or even legal consequences.

Defence Against the Problem

There are a number of steps that any organisation can take to defend against electronic mail-based attacks and embedded virus attacks in particular. These are a mixture of technical steps and personal practices.

It is important for every organisation to ensure that their email server and client software is kept up to date. New attacks develop regularly and the defence against some of these attacks sometimes requires a software upgrade. Furthermore, modern email servers offer facilities such as content control and arbitrary message routing based on information about known sources of attack.

Likewise, a modern firewall, possibly coupled with a proxy server, will allow effective content scanning for known attack signatures. These components can prevent malicious payloads from being delivered to sensitive systems.

Equally important is the use of effective anti-virus software. There are a number of reputable vendors around. Some sites have reported that they have obtained the most effective defence against virus attacks by using software from multiple vendors rather than just relying on a single vendor. The software will be used most effectively if it is used at every entry point onto the network. This includes

> **TIP**
> Anti-virus software should be used in a continuous monitoring mode on servers and workstations

electronic mail, network downloads, portable media – even commercial software distributions. The software should also be used in a continuous monitoring mode on servers and workstations.

Additionally, this kind of software typically requires updating when a new attack occurs (by adding a new "attack signature" to the appropriate configuration files). The signatures are typically available from the vendor very soon after the emergence of a new attack.

> **TIP**
>
> If an email sender is not familiar, make sure that an anti-virus program has scanned any attachments

When reading email, consider the content of the message and the identity of the sender. If the sender is familiar, consider whether the content of the message is something the sender is likely to have intentionally sent. If not, then it's possible that the message was a forgery or was sent by a person or program mimicking the sender. In these cases, be careful of opening any attachments without checking whether they may be malicious (in fact, this applies to all cases). Likewise, if the sender is not familiar, make sure that an anti-virus program has scanned any attachments.

Many organisations often exchange documents internally or with other outside parties, which are commonly in formats understood by popular application packages such as Microsoft Word. When exchanging Word and other similar documents, exchange them in Rich Text Format (RTF) format if possible. Files that are in RTF format do not contain macros and therefore the possibility of a macro-virus attack is removed. Be careful that files with a .rtf extension are actually true RTF files. When using popular PC-based applications such as Microsoft Word, Excel and Powerpoint, consider disabling macros by default. Your system administrator should be able to assist if necessary.

Every organisation and user should ensure that effective backups are kept. Individual data backups taken at regular intervals and comprehensive software and configuration backups help to ensure that if a virus or email attack is successful, any damage can be overcome relatively quickly. Any doubts or suspicions should be reported to an appropriate system administrator, who should be able to check any suspicious messages or files for potential problems.

The Lesson

This article outlines some of the risks associated with services like electronic mail. These risks are real and in some cases the effect of an incident can be profound. There is no such thing as a "bulletproof network". However, a sensible attitude, coupled with commonsense precautions, can ensure that the advantages of networked technology can be obtained with minimal risk.

Survey – Melissa Virus

In 1999, AusCERT conducted a survey among its membership in the wake of the Melissa virus outbreak. The survey responses indicated that generally Melissa did not have a significant impact on most sites. Most failed to become infected and of those that did (about one in four), the impact was typically considered minimal (no more than several hours for recovery). Most sites did detect the virus but did not suffer any significant damage due to measures already in place.

As a result of the publicity surrounding Melissa, many sites reported taking the opportunity to update their anti-virus software. A number of these sites reported that while the newer software didn't pick up any Melissa problems, it did identify a number of other viruses which hadn't been found using previous earlier versions of the software, some of which were only a few weeks out of date. This reinforces the general recommendation of ensuring that anti-virus software is regularly updated.

Some sites reported that they had greater problems with other viruses such as Happy99 than they did with Melissa. For sites which were not directly infected but which noted a significant amount of increased workload, the major causes seemed to be disseminating information to their users, fielding enquiries about the virus and getting and installing anti-virus updates.

References

ICSA 1999 Computer Virus Prevalence Survey, available from
http://www.icsa.net/services/consortia/anti-virus/survey_request.shtml
Computer Crime and Security Survey 1999, available from
http://www.deloitte.com.au/downloads/Computer_Crime99.pdf
Viruses, Hoaxes and Trojan Horses, available from
http://www.auscert.org.au/Information/Sources/virus.html
AusCERT Advisory Index, available from
http://www.auscert.org.au/Information/Advisories/indexed
Frequently Asked Questions About the Melissa Virus, available from
http://www.cert.org/tech_tips/Melissa_FAQ.html
Frequently Asked Questions About the CIH Virus, available from
http://www.cert.org/tech_tips/CIH_FAQ.html
Internet Hoaxes, available from
http://ciac.llnl.gov/ciac/CIACHoaxes.html

Rob McMillan is senior security analyst with the Australian Computer Emergency Response Team (AusCERT). AusCERT's mission is to support and improve community awareness, representation and communication regarding computer security, both locally and internationally, by being the leading source of impartial and reliable computer security information and expertise. http://www.auscert.org.au

How a Virus Called Melissa Crippled a Government

More than 14,000 South Australian Government Department and agency workers had their internet access and inter-agency and external email facilities suspended in 1999 after a rapidly-replicating computer virus invaded the government's IT system.

Internet and email services were suspended for almost 24 hours while IT workers in the South Australian Department of Administration and Information Systems disinfected the virus and installed filtering software.

Melissa invaded Microsoft-based software programs and replicated itself, sending an often paralysing flood of essentially empty emails throughout an organisation.

Trevor Wynne, team leader for the department's South Australian Government Electronic Messaging System (SAGEMS), which acts as a gateway for all departments and agencies, said the department had cut net access and outside email facilities, though departments and agencies were still able to email within their own organisation.

Of around 12,500 emails queued to come into the SAGEMS, 12 contained Melissa viruses. Those replicated and forwarded themselves to staff. "Our strategy was to educate users not to open the files, advise them what we were doing and filter out the virus. Some agencies were able to use the system by Monday night and the rest were online the next day," said Wynne. Some of the department's servers had up to 2,000 users and coped "very well".

SOURCE: E-Commerce Today, Issue 36, March 31, 1999.
http://www.ecommercetoday.com.au

How to Stop Virus
Disasters at Server Level

Computer viruses have been a constant thorn in the side of IT managers for a long time, according to Kenny Liao, country manager of Trend Micro in Australia /New Zealand. The 1998 Virus Prevalence Survey carried out by the International Computer Security Association (ISCA) found that 99% of surveyed companies had experienced a virus attack.

In the 1999 survey, the group of 300 organisations had 263,784 virus encounters on PCs during 1997 and February 1999. About 43% of the respondents had experienced a virus disaster. More than half the respondents had encountered viruses sent via email in their disasters. About a quarter of respondents had experienced infections due to diskettes infected at home and then brought to work. Not only was valuable time lost in trying to remedy the virus (the average response was five person days for recovery), but the estimated costs ranged from over $A5000 to $A100,000.

Underestimating Virus Damage

"Viruses are doing more damage to businesses than most employees realise," says Liao. This is particularly evident in a recent survey by Morgan & Banks Technology (MBT). The report claims that expanding internet use and the rise of e-commerce are the main culprits of virus infection. In fact, 53% of firms reported that they had caught viruses off the internet or from email.

Twenty-four percent of the MBT survey respondents said that they lost work due to infection, which is unacceptable to most, if not all, employers. In some cases, companies were able to identify the source of infection, however there has never been a successful legal case dealing with these issues.

Action Plan – Try Server Anti-Virus Products

Organisations have to stop viruses at the email and internet server level. This is quicker and more cost-effective than trying to clean up every desktop within the organisation, once the virus has contaminated them. Trend Micro anti-virus products are specifically designed to stop the virus at the server level before it gets to the desktops," says Liao. Trend Micro's products include InterScan VirusWall which detects and removes viruses from inbound and outbound SMTP mail and attachments, FTP and HTTP traffic in real time. It also blocks malicious or unsigned Java applets and ActiveX objects and prevents spammers from using your SMTP server to relay bulk email.

InterScan eManager blocks unsolicited email (spam), automatically downloads updated spam source lists, controls distribution of sensitive email content, schedules email deliveries to optimise network bandwidth and charts email traffic patterns.

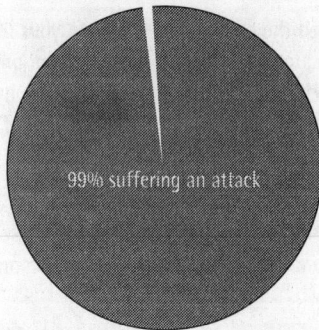

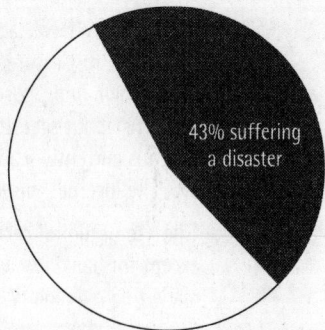

99% suffering an attack

43% suffering a disaster

The 1998 Virus Prevalence Survey carried out by the International Computer Security Association (ISCA) found that 99% of surveyed companies had experienced a virus attack. About 43% of the respondents had experienced a virus disaster. More than half the respondents had encountered viruses sent via email in their disasters. In fact, 53% of firms reported that they had caught viruses off the internet or from email.

This article was provided by Trend Micro, makers of anti-virus software products. http://www.trendmicro.com.au

Why Encrypting Email is Vital

By Lia Timson

I f you have never activated the encryption button on your Microsoft Outlook Express, rest assured you are not alone. For email encryption is a largely yet-unknown and unused facility in internet communications, despite widespread concerns about security and privacy. In fact, according to the Canadian Government, which is currently leading the encryption movement, 99% of all email traffic travels over the internet unsecured.

"The use of digital certification in general in the commercial sector is fairly minimal, except for banking, defence and government," says Peter Moore, Microsoft senior marketing manager Windows.

Moore is unable to tell what percentage of Microsoft users have actually deployed their encryption facilities or where to go to obtain the digital certification necessary to activate them. "We just have to have it as a standard feature or we couldn't be considered by banks and government (contracts)," he says.

According to Microsoft, before you can send encrypted messages, you must also obtain a digital ID for each recipient. They should be able to send it to you if they have one. But the fact is most businesses and individuals within them don't.

Jonathan Poole, head of internet services at Westpac, says that is why the bank has opted for controlling the format through which it receives emails from online customers. "When customers send us information through the site they must use a standard form (ie: "contact us") so we control the content of the message. It is then routed to an operator through an intelligent email management system and is encrypted to secure authenticity and security," he says.

While online transactions such as funds transfers are secured by 128-bit encryption, standard emails are secured by 40-bit encryption. "Most of the time we are not getting sensitive data through (email). It is just prudence to ensure the channel is secure," Poole says, whilst indicating that 128-bit capacity will be adopted for all email by next June nevertheless.

John Rolland, general manager internet services at Telstra agrees. "More and more companies and professionals are getting online, but don't currently understand the open nature of the internet and the need to encrypt. There are lots of instances of emails going astray or being sent to the wrong address. It creates problems on a global basis, but there are no global standards to solve them."

Anything of a confidential nature such as tender documents and other commercially sensitive data, as well as of a personal nature such as health records must be encrypted, he says. "It does reduce risks of breaches depending on the program used," he adds.

And there are more than 800 encryption programs available today, some of which are untested, according to the information and privacy commissioner in Ontario, Canada. The agency offers the following advice: "If your company is in the market for an email encryption product, ensure the code has been tested, that it has been in use for at least three years and is easy to use."

"Encryption is still the key (to internet security)," says Westpac's Poole, "but at the end of the day it is time-consuming and complicated for the user. It's a challenge the whole industry faces."

Lia Timson is a freelance journalist based in Sydney. She is a regular contributor to E-Commerce Today newsletter and magazine. http://www.ecommercetoday.com.au

Security High on the Business Agenda

A survey carried out by Content Technologies in 1999 shows that about 45% of surveyed organisations intend implementing technology to prevent breaches of confidential information within 12 months. Combined with the 20% of organisations which already do so, the figure will rise to 65% in the year 2000.

The survey was based on responses from 46 organisations which use Content Technologies' MIMEsweeper, a leading solution for email and web content security. The survey was conducted during an interactive webcast held by Content Technologies Asia/Pacific to launch MIMEsweeper 4.0.

"Most organisations lose information through mistakes, but some lose very sensitive information through deliberate acts," says Alan Schaverien, the managing director of leading content security firm Content Technologies Asia/Pacific. "Now that almost all organisations use email, they are finding they also need to plug security leaks."

	Implemented now	Not now, but by 2000	Total by 2000
Prevent Viruses	96%	0%	96%
Email Abuse	61%	20%	81%
Disclaimers / Messages	50%	25%	75%
Confidentiality Breaches	20%	45%	65%
Control Files / Bandwidth	31%	29%	60%
Prevent Spoof	19%	37%	56%
Prevent Spam	26%	29%	55%

SOURCE: Content Technologies Asia-Pacific.

The next fastest-growing requirement is preventing spoofed email, something 37% of respondents intend implementing within a year. Spoofing occurs when one email user assumes someone else's electronic identity. About 19% of respondents currently prevent spoofing and the figure will rise to 56% in 2000.

"Email is one of the basic tools of electronic commerce," says Schaverien. "But how can you safely do business with someone if they are assuming someone else's electronic identity?"

"Almost all organisations have problems with email," he says. "The only question is how bad that problem is. And this survey shows that new problems are emerging all the time."

While they are the fastest-growing new email content security problems, confidentiality breaches and spoofing rank behind virus prevention, preventing email abuse and adding legal disclaimers and corporate messages in terms of current usage.

About 96% of organisations surveyed use MIMEsweeper to prevent viruses, a figure not expected to change; 61% use it to prevent email abuse, forecast to rise to 81% in 2000 and 50% add disclaimers or corporate messages, forecast to rise to 75% in 2000.

In every category of content security, more than 50% of surveyed organisations expect to have implemented solutions by 2000. Other applications include controlling email attachment file sizes and managing network bandwidth (currently 31%, rising to 60% by 2000); and preventing spam email (currently 26%, rising to 55%).

"Screening out viruses and obscene messages is no longer enough," says Schaverien. "Email usage in the workplace is maturing very rapidly. As it becomes more and more mission-critical, a whole raft of content security problems need to be addressed."

This article was provided by Content Technologies which has 350 Asia-Pacific customers, with more than 350,000 protected corporate users. More than 250 organisations use MIMEsweeper in Australia alone, a number expected to double over the next 12 months. There are over 40 users in New Zealand.

Where to Find Email Encryption Products

Most email encryption products fall into two main standards or protocols – S/MIME V.3 and Open PGP. S/MIME V.3 stands for Secure Multipurpose Internet Mail Extension, Version 3. Open PGP stands for Open Pretty Good Privacy. In the tradition of competing ad hoc standards, they are incompatible and this situation is likely to continue.

S/MIME V.3 recently became an approved standard by the Internet Engineering Task Force (IETF). The IETF is currently working on also creating an Open PGP standard.

Having two incompatible standards is not a problem for a company that decides to use one protocol to communicate internally. But it does create a challenge for communicating securely with a host of external organisations or individuals that have opted to use incompatible products.

Apart from choosing which protocol to use, the consumer has to choose a product. That is where it gets complicated. The following is just a small sample of the various products available.

1. Web-based encryption services give the user an email account on a site and provide encryption software at that site. The site acts as a traffic controller for the user's email:

* http://www.ZipLip.com

* http://www.Hushmail.com

Using web-based systems is easy. Simply follow their instruction list. Be aware that some web-based email encryption systems require both the author and reader to register to the site to encrypt and decrypt email.

2. PC-based applications install on a user's PC or network:

* http://www.jawstech.com

* http://www.pgpi.com

* http://www.cypost.com

* http://www.ancort.ru/

* http://abi.hypermart.net

* http://www.invisimail.com

* http://www.cybergs.com/~issonline/

* http://www.symantec.com

Application-based tools vary in degrees of usability and strength. A good bet is to look for ones computer magazines have tested and given the coveted "editors" choice' stickers. Most of the current products have made encrypting email a one-or-two click process once the program has been setup. This is a major improvement from just a year ago. These PC-based products are independent of the Internet Service Provider used and can be installed with a few mouse clicks.

3. Public key infrastructures incorporate end-to-end security for organisations:

* http://www.entrust.com

* http://www.verisign.com

These solutions add a host of other services to basic email encryption ranging from securing sites to managing authentication. This includes handling all digital certificates (i.e., where a third party guarantees your identity) needed by an organisation to move information securely.

4. Hybrid applications have email encryption plus other features such as anonymizers/ pseudonymizers to break the connection between the user and any electronic flotsam that he or she leaves behind on the internet:

* http://www.zeroknowledge.com

* http://www.proxymate.com

The promising software "Freedom" by Zero Knowledge was at the beta stage of development as of August 1999 and, according to the company, it:

* Manages all digital identities necessary, watches all outbound traffic for personal information, automatically encrypts and routes traffic through their Freedom network, transparently decrypts all incoming traffic, manages cookies and filters spam.

Proxymate's services do not include email encryption but provide aliases. The service is easy to install and use. This proxy-based service gives users anonymity while surfing the net. Once registered (the software has an automatic setup option), the only added steps involve entering a username and password when you start up your Web browser. Proxymate provides aliases to sites asking for a user's name and email address. Essentially a privacy screen, the service is transparent to the user.

5. Encryption tools in Netscape Communicator and Internet Explorer involve purchasing a digital certificate (60-day-free-trial period) from a third party such as Verisign. Vendors have simplified and fully integrated the process for installation and use in the browsers. However, expect to pay $10-$20/year for your digital ID. Corporate rates are available as well.

The Product Checklist ✔

Once the user or organisation has done some fact-finding and is in the market for an email encryption product, keep the following things in mind.

1. Has the encryption code been tested?

This assumes that the code is available for testing. Untested code is dangerous, as Netscape can attest to with Communicator 4. Netscape has published its Communicator 5 code for testing. Yet not all companies do this. Third parties tied to academic cryptography bodies do the best testing. The Centre for Applied Cryptography at University of Waterloo, (http://www.cacr.math.uwaterloo.ca) is a fine Ontario example. In the words of Robert Morris Sr., former senior scientist at the American National Security Agency: "Never underestimate the time, expense and effort someone will expend to break a code."

2. Is it a mature encryption software?

Mature in this context means the software has been in use for at least three years, undergone testing and review and continues to be used. In 1997, PC Magazine reviewed several email encryption systems. Two years later, some of these products and their companies are impossible to find, or perhaps worse, might no longer exist.

3. Does it meet the needs of your organisation or personal preferences?

The user needs to assess whether the product can support the traffic of emails generated. He or she needs to decide whether the product provides the required protection needed. On the other hand, if the email content is of limited value to others, use a product like Pkzip. Pkzip is a commonly used utility to zip or compress files through symmetric encryption. A complex password might be sufficient.

Just change the password often and avoid file names that are too descriptive of the content, because that's another possible clue for snoopers.

4. What is the learning curve and ease of use of the product?

This often comes down to the number of key strokes it takes to encrypt and decrypt email. It also comes down to the steps and time needed to acquire digital certificates (a way to avoid the need to remember and manage multiple passwords.)

References

http://www.imc.org/smime-pgpmime.html
For a more in-depth review of the two protocols, please see an article by Dave Kosiur, on the zdnet Help Channel, April 28, 1999, entitled "Email Privacy": http://www.zdnet.com/zdhelp/. Finding this article is not straightforward. Once at the URL, type "email" into the search window and choose "Internet" in the "Categories" window. In the related info, click on Email Privacy (How to).
Note: the Information and Privacy Commission does not endorse any of the products listed, nor any other products. This list is for reference only.
http://www.netscape.com/security/basics/getpercert.html

This is an excerpt from the paper "Types of Email Encryption Products" produced by the Information and Privacy Commissioner of Ontario, Canada. http://www.ipc.on.ca

Need For Email to be Encrypted

The need for businesses to understand the importance of and techniques involved in encrypting electronic data was growing as email became more popular, says John Rolland, Telstra's GM for internet services.

More businesses are using email to transmit documents, such as contracts and service agreements, but they fail to take measures to make sure their documents are secure and confidential, he said. For these businesses, the risks involved with the electronic transmission of material were growing, he said.

"Small business users need to start to understand the importance of encrypting information if they are going to use email to send confidential material," he said.

Patrick Fair, a partner with Phillips Fox, Sydney, says while the risk of an email being intercepted was actually "quite small", emails could still be lost or misdirected.

This meant companies could be potentially liable for losses if they were at fault. He said businesses which traded with suppliers using an extranet had a responsibility to ensure their suppliers' competitors didn't see any information transmitted electronically.

SOURCE: E-Commerce Today, Issue 38, April 15, 1999.
http://www.ecommercetoday.com.au

Encrypted Email Up Close – Journey of a Message

By Jim Heath

John wants to send an email message to Herman, his contract manager in Germany. John types the message on his screen. When the message is worded the way John wants it, he clicks an encrypt option on the mailer software. It verifies the name of the person he wants to encrypt to – Herman – from a list of people that John has "public keys" for. The encryption software then automatically mixes and re-mixes every binary bit of the message with a key, then mixes that key with every binary bit in Herman's public key.

Result: A digital mess that can only be unscrambled by the same software, but by using Herman's private key. In Germany, the scrambled message pops up in Herman's email. He selects the "decrypt" option on his mailer. The software asks him for his passphrase. He types this in and that decrypts his private key (a very long number stored on his hard drive, which he doesn't have to remember or even look at). Enormous calculations then take place and Herman's software reverses the mess created by John's software. And John's original message appears on Herman's screen.

But what if John's message was intercepted by a hacker? It would do the hacker no good at all. It's hopeless to unscramble the message without Herman's private key, the hacker doesn't have that. And the hacker can't work out Herman's private key by knowing what his public key is. No-one can. Which is why the public key can safely be made public. It is theoretically possible to calculate the private key from the public key, but "computationally infeasible" (as cryptographers sincerely put it).

Even if the hacker ran the fastest computer on the planet to work on the calculation, his bones would be dust and the planet's continents in very different positions, yet still the calculation wouldn't be finished. (This is no exaggeration.)

And there's something else: If John wants to, he can add a "digital signature" to his message. It's like a mathematical watermark that can be checked by Herman's software. Herman can be sure that the message came from John, not from someone impersonating John. After all, anyone can send Herman an encrypted message using Herman's public key. That's what it's there for. Anyone could say they are John. But only John can digitally sign a message that can be verified by anyone who has John's public key.

The digital signature also proves the message hasn't changed a jot since John signed it. One extra blank space anywhere and Herman's software will tell him: "Bad signature." Digital signatures are as secure as the encrypted message itself. They can't be faked – not in any "computationally feasible" time.

Jim Heath is a director of Viacorp a Western Australia-based corporate writing company. This is an extract from an article "How Electronic Encryption Works and How it Will Change Your Business". www.viacorp.com

Email Security – Risks and Solutions

By Jim Heath

Password Protection is Not Enough

Some people try to protect their email messages by first saving them as word-processing files with a password. Then they send the word-processing files by email, as attachments. The concept is broadly right, but unfortunately, word-processing password systems are too weak for the realities of the internet. There are free password "crackers" that can break most of those password systems. If someone knows how to intercept your file, it's a good bet your password will soon be displayed on their computer screen.

In addition, a company in the US sells sophisticated software that cracks all the common business-application password systems: Microsoft Word, Excel and Money, WordPerfect, Lotus 123, Novell Netware and others. It's meant for business people who forget their passwords and need to re-open their "protected" files. But anyone can buy the cracking software.

Using pkzip for Email Security

A sounder approach is to use a password with the compression software pkzip. It is used to compress electronic files before they're sent across the internet. It also has a password protection system that's much stronger than the systems used in word processors.

Another advantage: Most people who have been using the internet for a while have a copy of pkzip. They need it to decompress files they download from the web. So there's no software to "set up". You and your email correspondent only need to agree on a password. Normally you do that over the phone or by fax, not by email!.

Important: Choose a messy password, 15 characters long or more. Use some uppercase and some lowercase letters, a few numbers and some punctuation. For example: uPP71$raNdommmiN,,,4a It's necessary to go to that trouble, instead of using an easy password like "zanzibar", because there are several pkzip password crackers on the internet and pkzip is regarded as low-level security by cryptographers. Be warned also that there is free software that will extract a pkzip password if you know (or can guess) a small but exact part of the message.

What You Can Do

Download a copy of pkzip and learn how to use the password system. One source is pkzip: http://www.pkware.com

> **TIP**
>
> A good browser system should be open for independent inspection by experts and have been used for a number of years without flaws

Using PGP for Email Security

Pretty Good Privacy (PGP) is encryption software first put together in 1991 by an American cryptographer, Phil Zimmermann. Then it was distributed free on the internet. For three years, he was under threat of prosecution by the US Government for exporting a "munition". The encryption system was so strong it was classified under cold-war rules as a weapon of war.

It is certainly a strong, well-tested and carefully reviewed system. Its workings are open for inspection and they always have been. It has been around for quite a long time. It passes all the practical tests. PGP is the best publicly-available system for sending electronic messages securely.

There are two drawbacks, but not imposing ones. Firstly, it has been an elite system, so it's unlikely to be found among the software of the business person you want to communicate with. You will probably have to encourage them to install it and learn how to use it. Secondly, it takes some learning, although PGP is no longer as hard to use, or hard to understand what's happening when you use it as before. There is a fat – but clear - manual with it. You can also use PGP to encrypt any electronic file. (So it's useful for a range of electronic security, other than just email messages.)

What You Can Do

Download a copy of PGP and read the manual. Then experiment with it, sending encrypted email. Source: http://www.pgpi.com

Using Web Browsers for Email Security

Some web browsers have built-in email encryption (for example, the system in Netscape's Messenger in Communicator 4.05 and Microsoft's Outlook Express in Internet Explorer 4.01). They use formidably strong encryption. What makes this useful for business communication is that browsers are everywhere. The person you want to send email to may already use one of these secure browsers. Which means you each have a ready-made and strong encryption system at your disposal.

At least in theory, browsers can give you good security. There's a pitfall Though in using browsers in Australia. The pitfall is those US export controls on strong encryption – the exported versions of the US browsers have their encryption systems drastically weakened. The encryption has been broken by students, for example, using the combined computing power from a network of PCs.

To counter that deliberate weakness, there are free software patches (upgrades) available from outside the US that return the browsers to full-strength encryption. One of these patches was developed in Australia.

Good browser systems should: be open for independent inspection by experts and: have been used for a number of years without flaws.

Which browsers pass those two tests?

None, yet. But in early 1998, Netscape published the source code for its Communicator 5.0 software. That opened the system for inspection and so it passes Test 1. Some UK and Australian cryptographers and programmers quickly added full-strength encryption to it. But their efforts haven't been time-tested for long enough (Test 2.).

So should you trust a browser to send secure email? If you simply want to keep the press from knowing too early about a new building you're moving to, then a browser's encryption is strong enough. If your company discovers a giant oilfield and you need to let your overseas offices know the details, you might hesitate to use a browser.

What You Can Do

Download a browser that has built-in email encryption and set it up. Learn to use it. Then monitor the internet for news about security flaws in it. If you hear no bad news, your confidence can gradually increase.

Jim Heath is a director of Viacorp a Western Australia-based corporate writing company. This is an extract from an article "Internet Security Risks and Solutions" reproduced courtesy of the Western Australian E-Commerce Centre: http://ecommercecentre.online.wa.gov.au. http://www.viacorp.com

Why Faxes Are Not Secure

By Jim Heath

The major security problems with faxes are obvious. Faxes are sometimes sent to the wrong number by mistake. The correct fax number can be transposed or the wrong number used. And there can also be disturbances in the telephone network that mysteriously connect faxes to the wrong number. A fax can also be read by anyone who happens to be near the fax machine. In some offices, the "need-to-know" principle reigns. But it's hard to enforce without giving all the key people a personal fax machine. Instead, people resort to phoning the person they want to fax, making sure they will be standing by the fax machine, then sending the fax.

However another security risk is less obvious - interception. A fax line can be bugged and all the faxes read - incoming and outgoing. Technically, it's easy to do. One prominent case was in 1990, when Japanese hackers were caught stealing information from US corporations by intercepting their faxes. And this is getting easier. These days, it's no problem to scan satellite or microwave links for fax messages. A bit of home-built equipment can monitor satellite traffic.

For someone who can spend more money, there are commercial fax interception units that can monitor up to 150 fax transmissions from a 6,000-line satellite. The risks from this broadband interception are severe. A company's faxes can be intercepted just because of the route they take through the common carriers - not because the company is a target for industrial spies or hackers. Satellite signals cross national borders. Faxes can be intercepted in nations with no privacy concerns.

Email Security Checklist

✔ Be sure of the strength of security used. There is a choice of security strengths available. If you are sending information of value, then be sure that your email system can secure with 128-bit DES keys.

✔ Consider the quality of security in the application itself. If possible, look for products that have been tested against the security standard ITSEC (Information Technology Security evaluation criteria).

✔ Use standards. There is a standard protocol for email security. This is called Secure Multipurpose Internet Mail Extensions (or S/MIME). Be sure to use a solution that supports the latest version of this standard.

✔ Know how to use secure email for e-commerce. When used in association with a public key infrastructure (or PKI), which provides digital certificates of identity, secure email systems can be used as the backbone of high value e-commerce systems. Be sure that your security allows this to happen.

✔ Be sure you have control over the system. Once you realise that secure email is as much about authentication as encryption, then you will realise that it is very important to manage users who have secure email. The security system needs to have some central administration in order to be certain that they are using the facility for valid purposes.

✔ Understand the alternative ways to secure your mail. There are two fundamentally different approaches on how to secure email. One is to secure the message at a users' desktop; the other involves securing messages as they leave the organisation or site. The one which is best depends on how your mail system is implemented today and how it may change in the future.

✔ Take your time to decide. Consider the overall future use of secure email, as well as the immediate demand, so select a solution that will provide the service you require in future years, as well as now.

These tips provided by Baltimore Technologies. Baltimore specialises in the development and marketing of a products and services to secure business conducted via computer networks, whether for internet, extranet or intranet applications. http://www.baltimore.com

Top Email Security Hurdles Faced by Businesses

1. Breaches of confidentiality

Most organisations lose information via email through mistakes, but some lose very sensitive information through deliberate or malicious acts.

2. Inappropriate email usage

Business email systems can be used for sexual, racial or other forms of harassment – for which employers may be liable – or other antisocial or illegal activities.

3. Spoof attacks

Spoofing is where the sender of an email can easily assume another identity in order to obtain confidential information.

4. E-pornography

Pornography is not only accessible via internet browsers, it can be distributed via email and often finds its way onto business email systems.

5. Email-borne viruses

Earlier destructive viruses spread through floppies or downloaded software but the latest viruses, like Melissa, are email attachments that spread at light speed over the Internet.

6. Network congestion and spam

Massive email attachments often associated with office jokes or pranks multiply like rabbits and can slow the network down to a snail's pace. Spam, or unsolicited email, is a major annoyance.

7. Liability for email usage

Employers may be found liable for the actions of their employees and this extends to their use of email, whether it is work-related or not. Even casual conversations may constitute contracts.

8. Copyright infringement

Distributing any copyright material via email may constitute making an infringing reproduction thereby breaching copyright.

9. Cyberwoozle threats

Program code disguised within emails can siphon information off users' PCs or the corporate network and send it out over the Internet.

These tips provided by Content Technologies Asia/Pacific.
http://www.mimesweeper.com.au

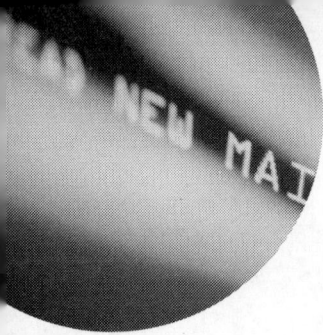

How to Fix Business Email Problems ✓

1. Introduce a security awareness culture

Regularly review your written procedures for monitoring content security threats and make sure they are communicated effectively. Produce a simple policy booklet to highlight the company's policy for email and encryption usage. If possible, make this part of a legally binding agreement, for example a contract of employment. To supplement this, conduct a short training course to ensure the message had been digested and to allow for any questions and feedback from employees. Produce posters to display on office premises so that employees are reminded of the policy. Overall, make your security statements clear, timely and achievable.

2. Be proactive with emails and stop anti-social behaviour

Take time to analyse incoming and outgoing emails and adjust and manage your policy to suit, using content security software. Are there certain file types or attachments that are causing problems? Does a specific supplier's emails cause problems? Are your employees sending emails with undesirable attachments or received files from non-business related sources? They could be violating your company email policy and leaving you open to key business security risks and corporate liability.

3. Protect your organisation from spam and spoof

Check you have set up your solution to detect the commonly-used spam phrases already included such as "free", "reply within 30 days" and "100% guaranteed".

Ensure your software can perform reverse address look-ups. RFC2505 "Anti-spam Recommendations for SMTP MTAs" recommends that products should be able to verify the source address of the email address, to check the validity of the site.

4. Regularly review blacklist sites

There are many sites on the World Wide Web that aim to help companies keep abreast of the newest threats in viruses, spamming techniques and less-than-desirable web sites. In order to maintain your spam list, take out a subscription to a spam blacklist site so you are automatically notified of new threats. There are organisations that offer a real-time service listing spam-hosts, for example VIX, IMRSS and ORBS.

5. Maintain your supplier relationships

Make sure you have installed the most appropriate content security system to manage the threat of malicious content. Make sure you are running the latest release of your content security software. Make sure you are running the latest release of your anti-virus software and have the most up-to-date virus signatures.

6. Maintain user lists

Make sure you delete the user rights of personnel who have left the company. Make sure you regularly review the user rights for individuals, groups and departments.

6. Review email disclaimers

Is your general company email disclaimer up to date? Are your individual and department disclaimers up to date? Have you reviewed your disclaimer with legal advisors to ensure you are maximising the protection of the company and employees?

8. Update your risk analysis regularly

Regularly analyse areas of your business which require differing levels of information security controls. Identify which areas are most prone to attack and take the necessary action.

9. Be a good internet citizen

Of course, policy should apply to your outgoing, as well as your incoming communications, so check that internally you can: Check outgoing email against your spam detectors Stop relaying data to external sites (anti-relay) Inform virus senders of their problem Scan all outgoing mail for viruses and virus hoaxes.

These tips provided by Content Technologies Asia/Pacific.
http://www.mimesweeper.com.au

Hotmail's Tips for Safe and Savvy Email

TIP

Maintain a healthy dose of scepticism

- Change your password often. To help ensure that your password is safe, change it often and use a strong password – one that includes both letters and numbers, which make it harder to break.

- Do not share your password. Most email administrators will not ask for your password; Hotmail will never ask for it. If you get a message from someone purporting to be from your ISP or email provider asking for your password, do not respond. This is a well-known, but rarely-used trick designed to fool users. As a rule, never share your password with anyone.

- Don't open attachments from anyone you don't know. Exercise caution with attachments and never open those from unknown sources.

- Log out. Logging out of an email account when finished can save you from rare but harmful security breaches. When using web-based email, be sure to log out of your account rather than simply pointing your browser to a new web page.

- Don't respond to spam. Responding to unsolicited mail only confirms that you have an active email address and this could open you up to further solicitation and scams that can clog your email inbox. Forward spam to the customer service department of the source's email provider (usually the address is something like abuse@[implicateddomain].com) and to uce@ftc.gov to alert the Federal Trade Commission. To help control spam, Hotmail provides members with "filters" for incoming mail. These can easily be set up to send certain messages (such as those that include particular words) directly to your online trash can.

- Keep your browser and internet software updated. Browsers such as Microsoft Internet Explorer often provide updates that deliver enhanced security features and bug fixes that sometimes offer increased protection.

- Use a secure network. If your email is part of a secure network, you are protected by administrators who watch for potential security problems and act to safeguard you from "hackers" (malicious users) who may try to steal personal information transferred through the network. Use caution with any unfamiliar network.

- Use common sense. Be smart when you're on the internet and maintain a healthy dose of scepticism. Use caution when revealing personal information such as your physical address to anyone you meet in cyberspace, even if they claim to be someone of authority. Do not be duped by emails asking for your password.

These tips provided by Hotmail, a leading free web-based electronic mail service, with over 23 million members. Hotmail was acquired by Microsoft in December 1997. To get a copy of these tips and other updates consumers can send a blank email to securitytips@hotmail.com. http://www.hotmail.com.au

Don't Forget Your Email Insurance

By Lia Timson

Most companies could be forgiven for spending most of their time concerned about how to crack the ever-enlarging internet marketplace and not giving much thought to insurance. Particularly email insurance.

Whilst ripples are beginning to be felt in the defamation and intellectual property insurance markets, where businesses publishing electronic material are concerned they are not infringing others' rights – or having their own assaulted, email insurance is yet to attract a following here and overseas.

Matthew Norris, underwriter at Hiscox Insurance Services, a syndicate of the London-based conglomerate Lloyd's, says although interest is growing, current email insurance enquiries are mostly confined to "lots of conversation".

"My own suspicion is that so many companies are struggling with the commercial and security issues in going onto the internet that their attention has been taken away from buying insurance," Norris says.

New Products Coming On-Stream

Hiscox markets a cyberliability product offering protection against internet and email liability, including the misuse of digital signatures. It is available in Australia, but no figures on uptake are available. Australian insurers are yet to launch such specific products, but some, such as HIH Winterthur, say they cover email risks as part of their information technology policies, which in this case are offered by the FAI division.

IT insurance specialist Dexta Corporation is also working on specific policies. Managing director Ashraf Kahma says a user-friendly product aimed at small and medium-sized enterprises will be available in late January or early February.

"Most business know they have some exposure, but are not sure if they are covered [by other all encompassing policies] for them or not. At least a minimum amount should be provided for if somebody sues a small business for defamation because an employee makes some derogatory comments in an email," Kahma says.

Not having such cover may mean the end of business just to cover prohibitive defence legal costs.

Roisin McGrady, professional risk manager with Sydney brokerage firm GSA Insurance, says most activity in the Australian market has been on the part of IT companies and internet service providers. She says a telecommunications multimedia policy, covering everything from local and long distance telephone calls to satellite and email communications, provides cover including breach of confidentiality, defamation and infringement of intellectual property.

Australian Market Set to Grow

> **TIP**
> Businesses need to decide where the risks for their organisations really lie. They need to decide how much they are potentially likely to lose and insure that.

"The Australian market is definitely there. We're very open to the use of the internet and new technologies. A lot of insurers will be launching (specific products) in the new year," McGrady says. In the meantime, businesses need to query their present policies and their e-commerce capabilities to decide where the risks for their organisations really lie," she adds. "They need to decide how much they are potentially likely to lose and insure that."

Norris agrees: "The first lines of defence are undoubtedly good business practice – good systems to avoid employee fraud and technological tools such as firewalls and encryption. However, next in line comes good legal practice like employee contracts, website representation, formation of electronic contracts and insurance.

"No system can ever be fully secure. If you have spent time and money making your system as secure as is reasonable, it would seem an omission not to fill the gap with a good insurance policy to mop up the problems your system cannot cope with."

Lia Timson is a freelance journalist based in Sydney. She is a regular contributor to E-Commerce Today newsletter and magazine. http://www.ecommercetoday.com.au